PIANO · VOCAL · GUITAR

switchfoot

THE BEST YET

www.switchfoot.com

ISBN 978-1-4234-6627-7

HAL•LEONARD®
CORPORATION

7777 W. BLUEMOUND RD. P.O. BOX 13819 MILWAUKEE, WI 53213

Visit Hal Leonard Online at
www.halleonard.com

DARE YOU TO MOVE

Words and Music by
JONATHAN FOREMAN

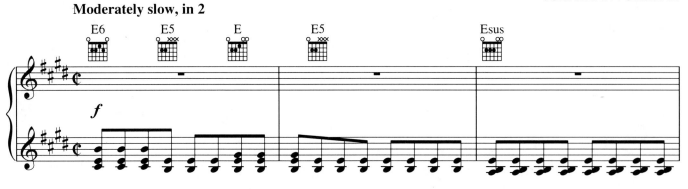

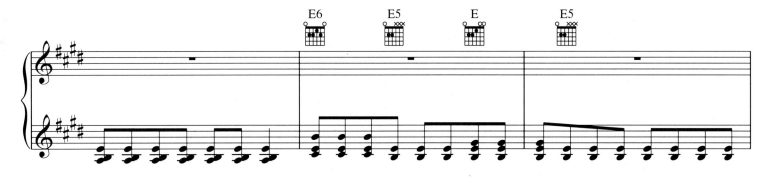

Wel-come to the plan - et. _____

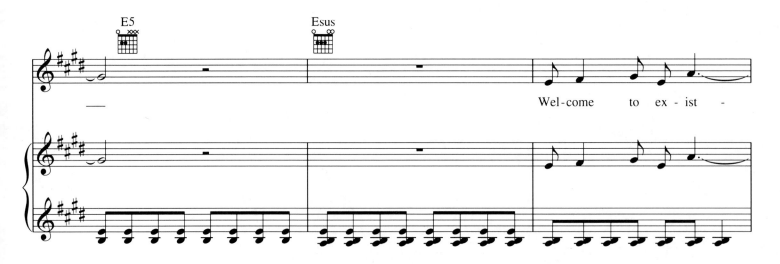

Wel-come to ex - ist -

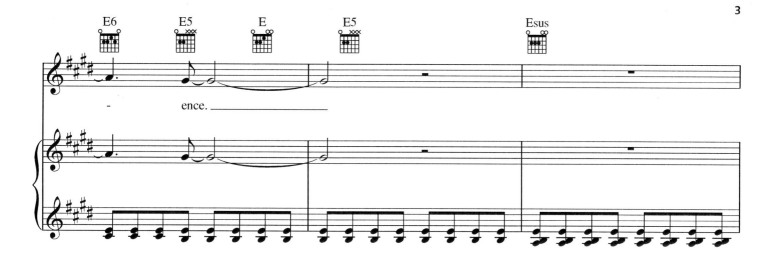

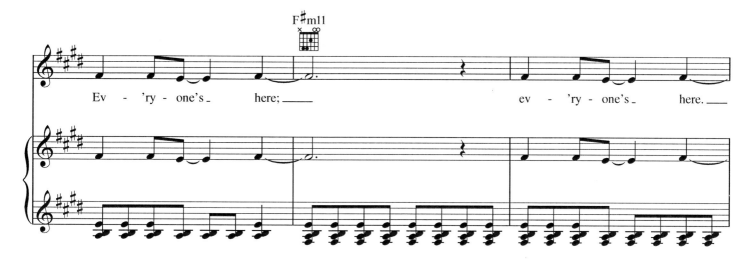

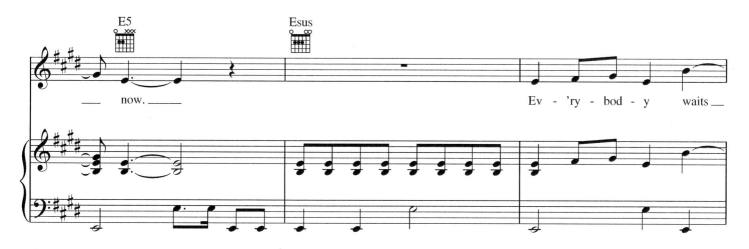

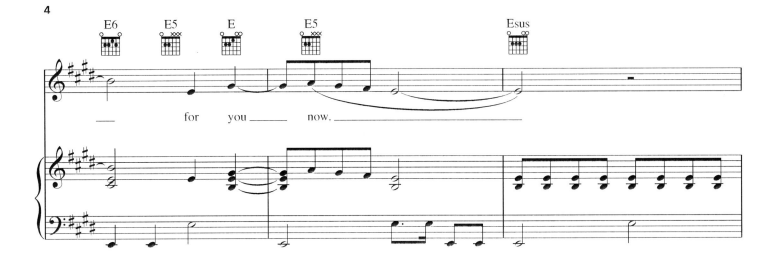

for you _____ now. _____

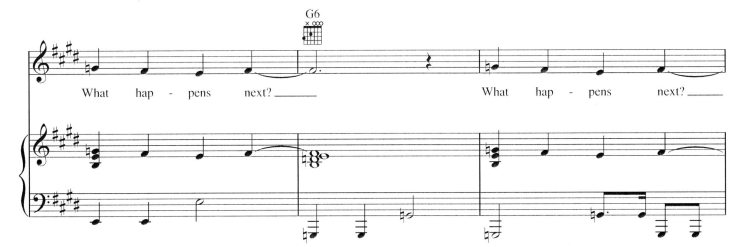

What hap - pens next? _____ What hap - pens next? _____

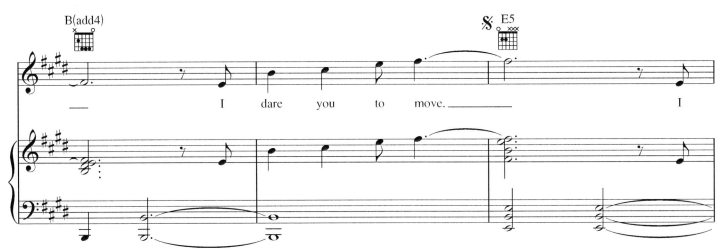

I dare you to move. _____ I

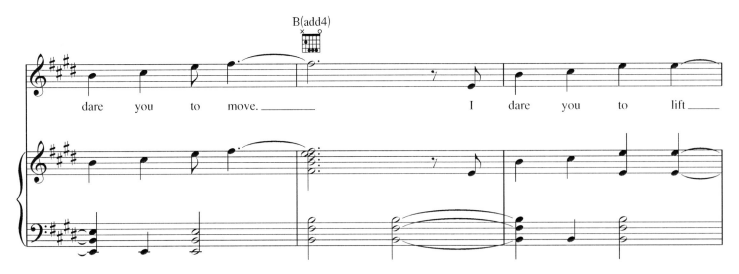

dare you to move. _____ I dare you to lift _____

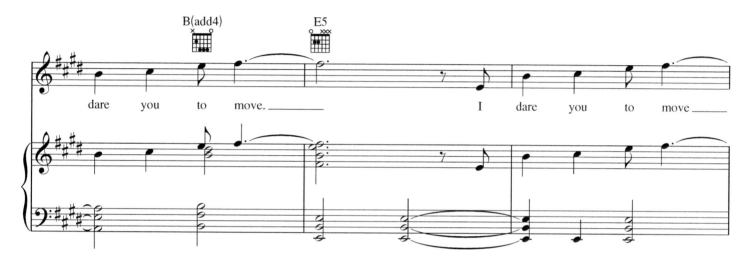

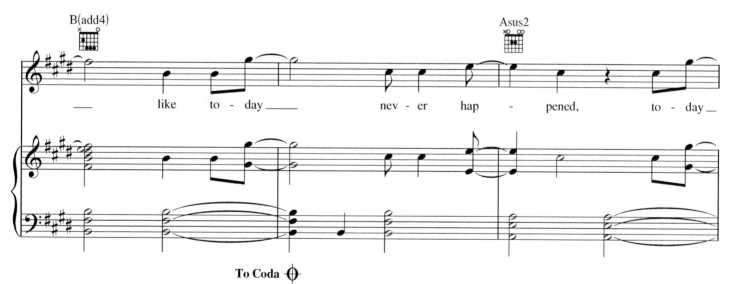

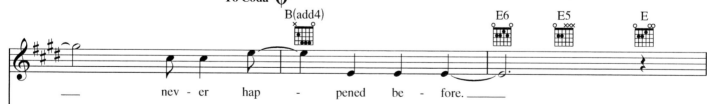

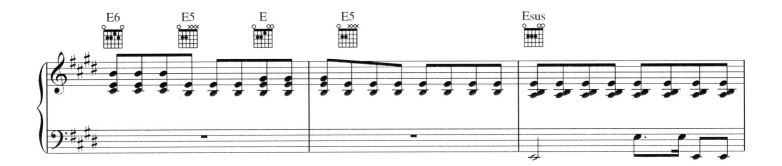

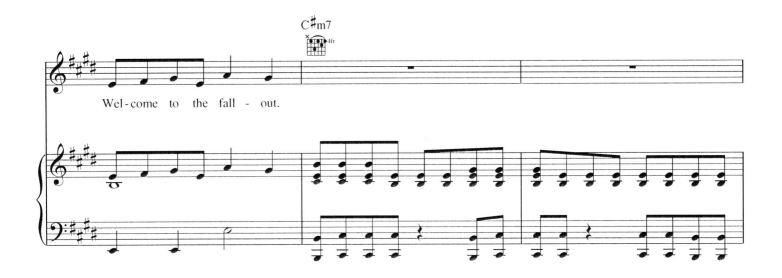

Wel-come to the fall - out.

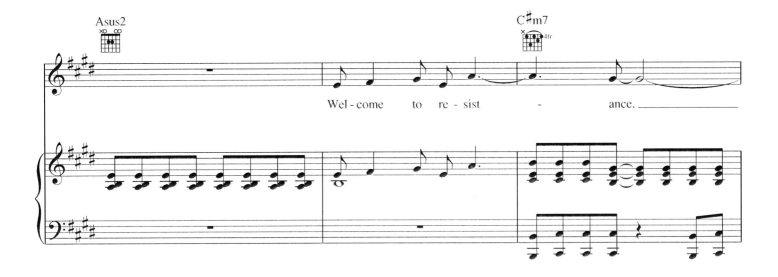

Wel-come to re-sist - ance.

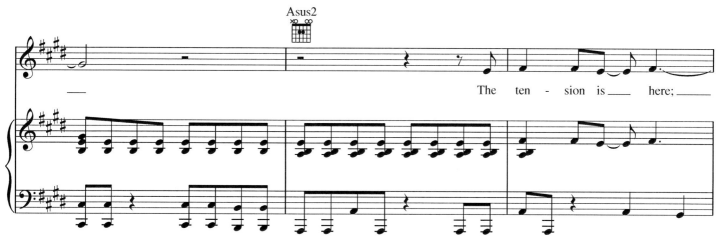

Asus2

The ten - sion is ___ here; ___

F#m11   Asus2

the ten - sion is ___ here ___

C#m7

be - tween who ___ you are ___ and who ___ you could be,

Asus2   F#m11

be - tween how ___ it is ___ and how ___ it should

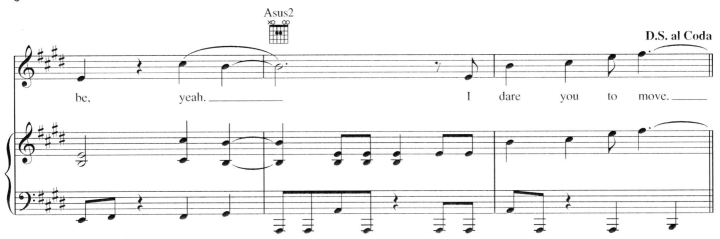

be, yeah. _____ I dare you to move. _____

-pened. May - be re - demp - tion has sto -

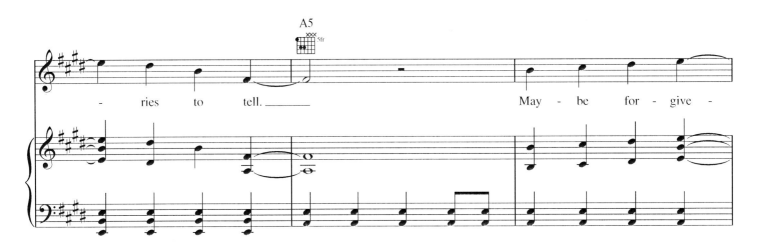

-ries to tell. _____ May - be for - give -

-ness is right _____ where you fell. _____

Where can you run _____ to es - cape _____ from your - self? ____

____ Where you gon - na go? _____

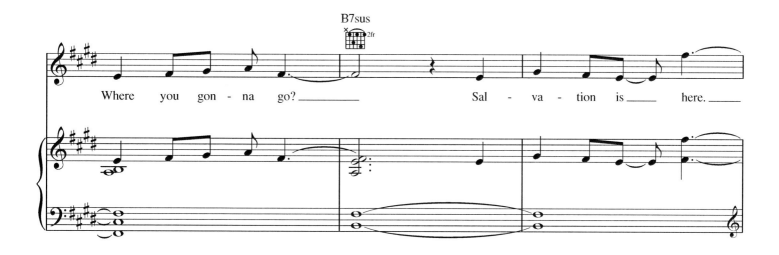

Where you gon - na go? _____ Sal - va - tion is ____ here. ____

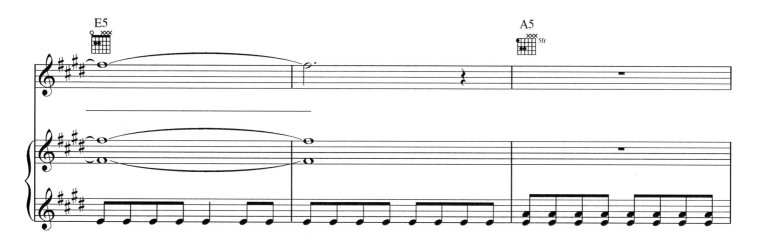

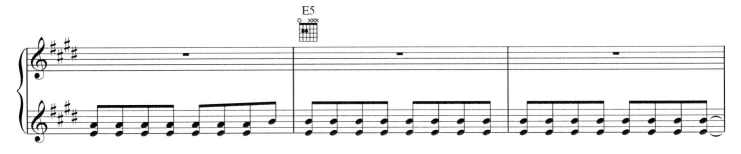

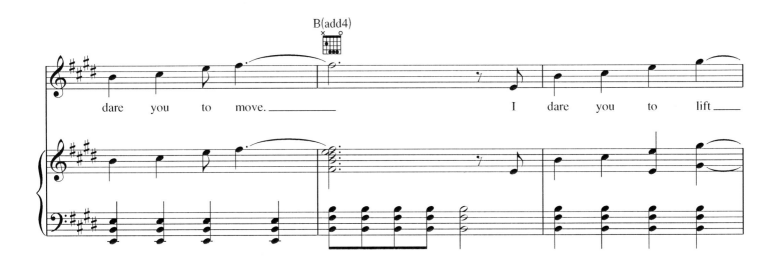

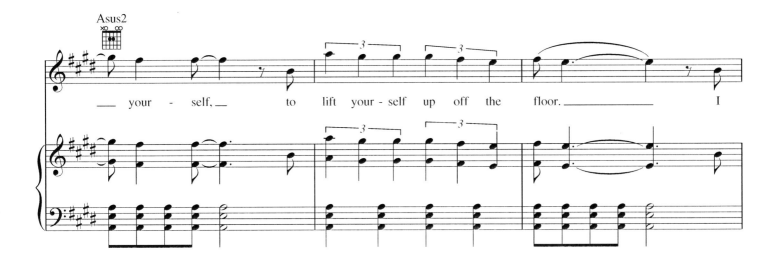

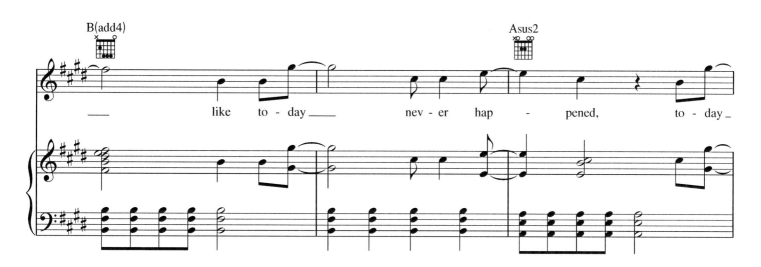

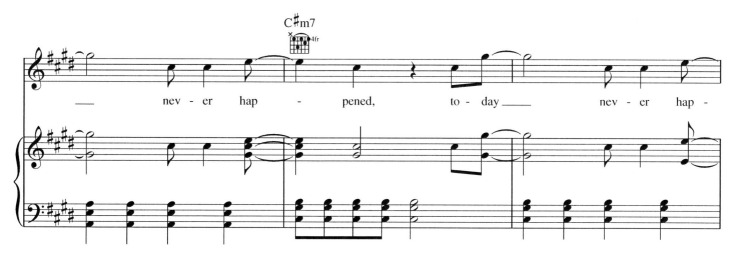

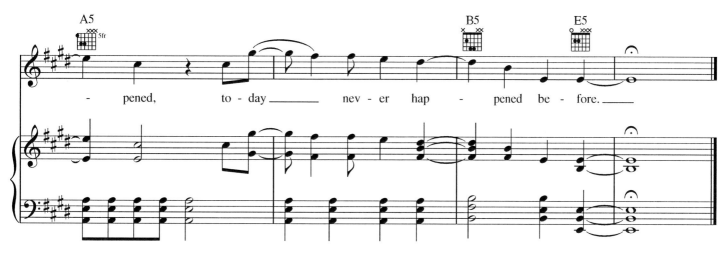

MEANT TO LIVE

Words and Music by JONATHAN FOREMAN
and TIM FOREMAN

Heavy Rock

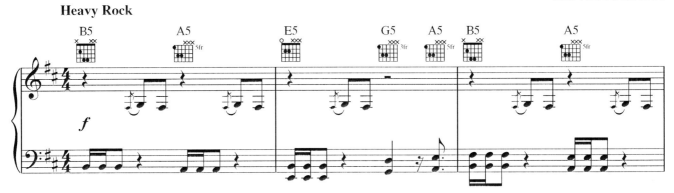

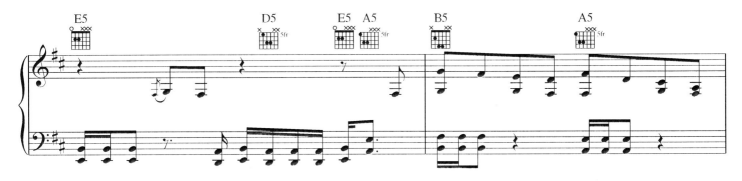

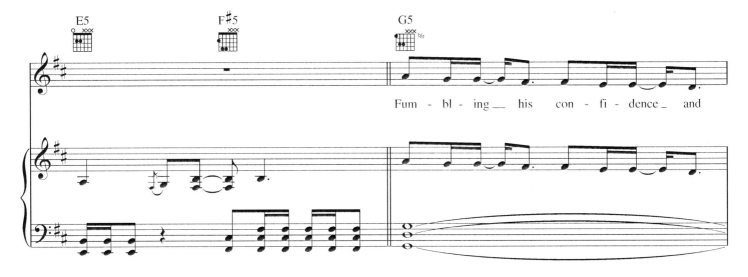

Fum - bl - ing __ his con - fi - dence __ and

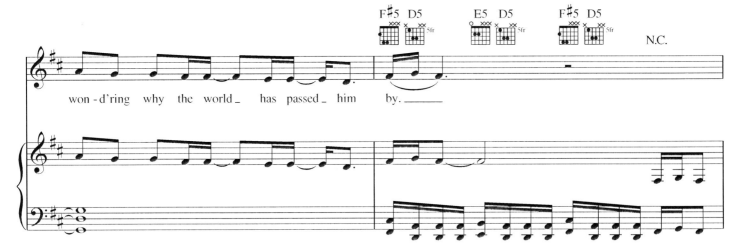

won - d'ring why the world __ has passed __ him by. ____

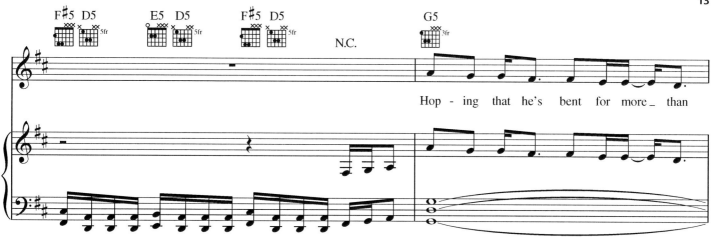

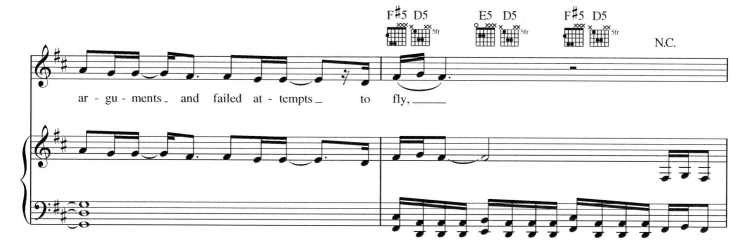

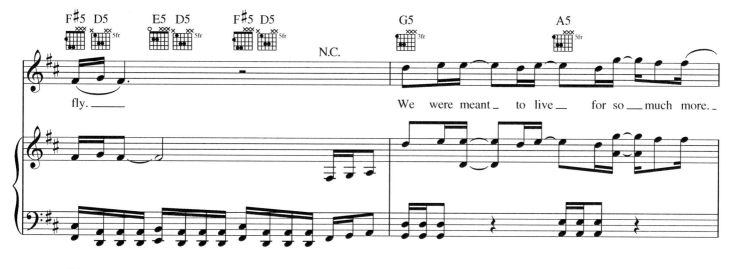

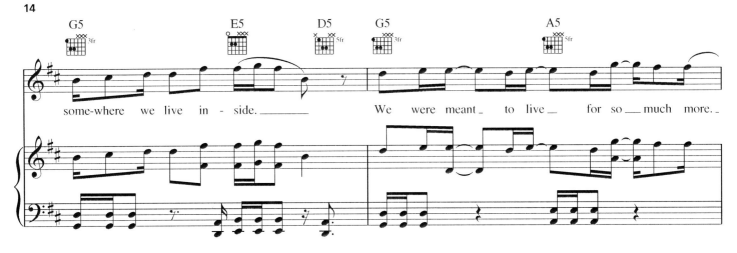

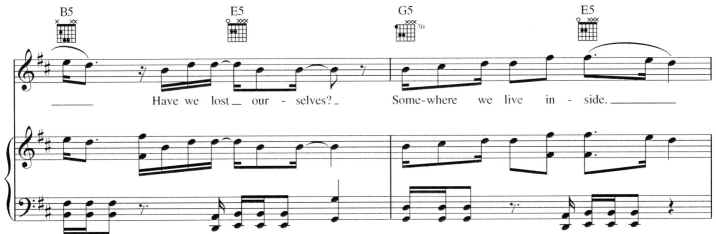

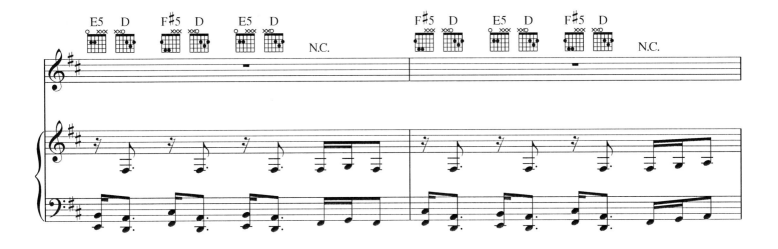

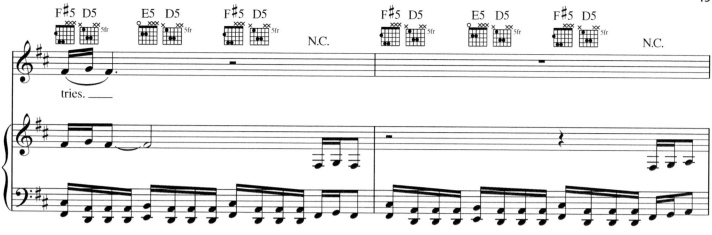

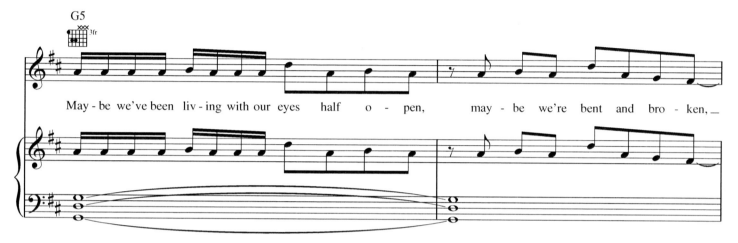

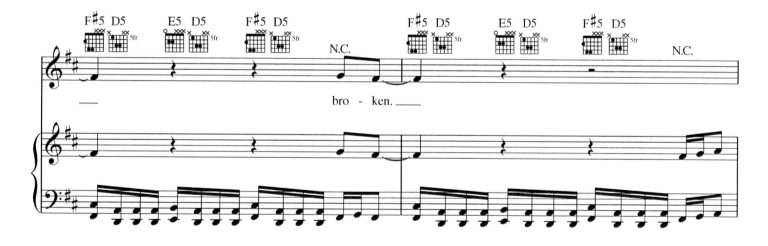

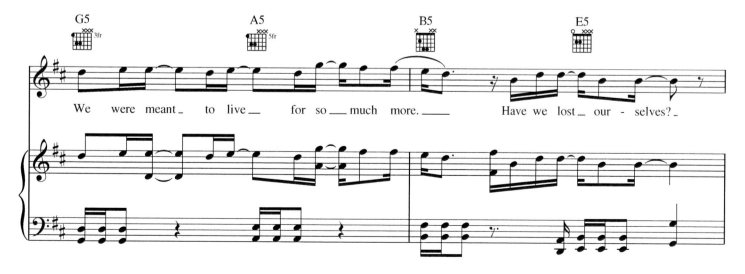

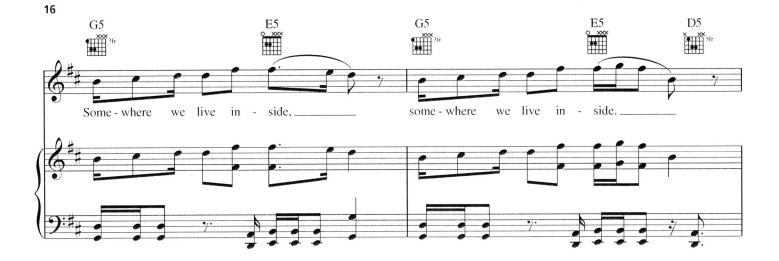

Some-where we live in-side,_____ some-where we live in-side._____

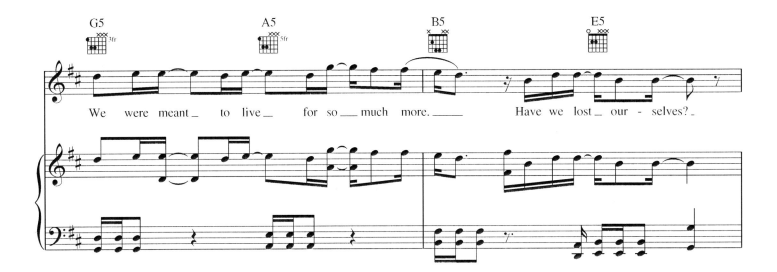

We were meant__ to live__ for so__ much more._____ Have we lost__ our - selves?__

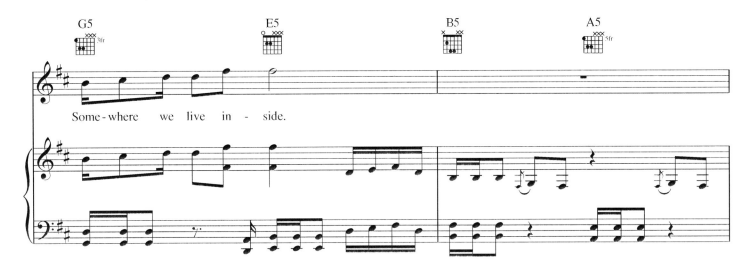

Some - where we live in - side.

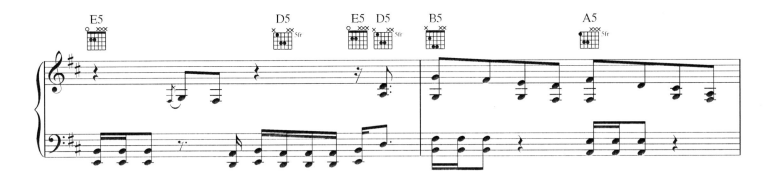

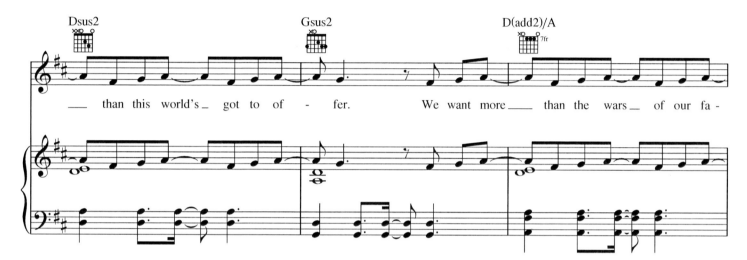

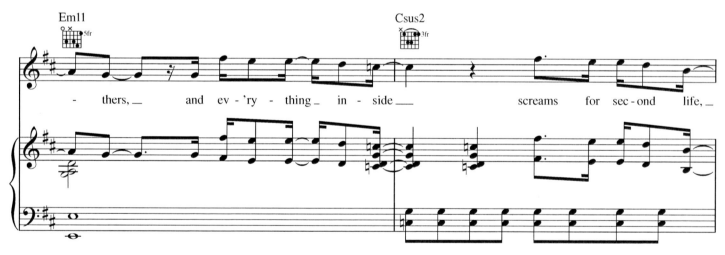

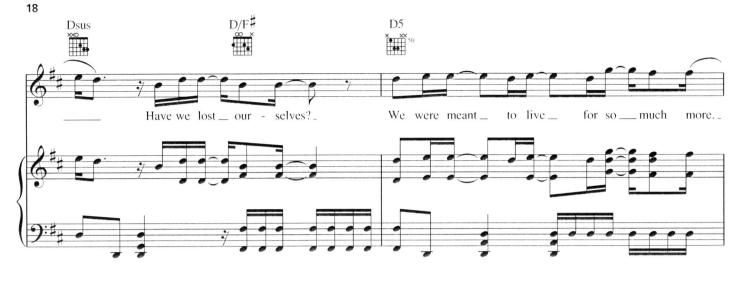

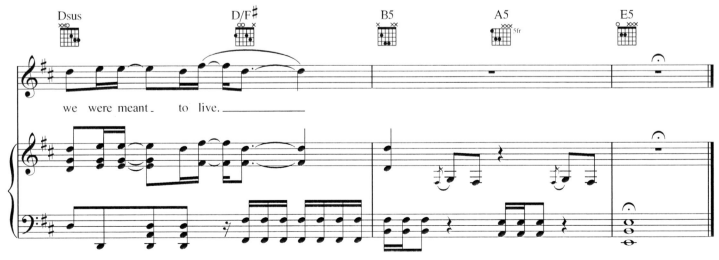

OH! GRAVITY

Words and Music by JONATHAN FOREMAN
and TIM FOREMAN

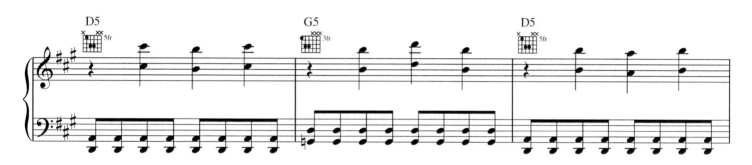

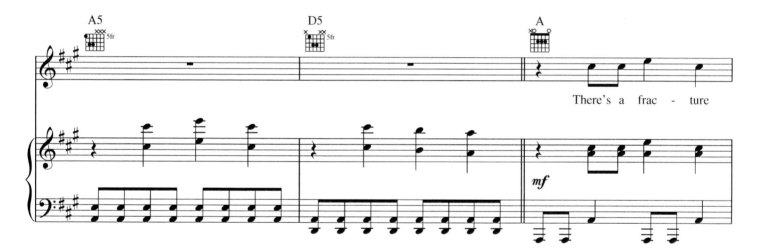

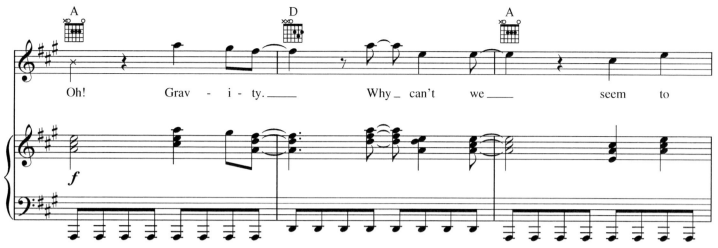

Oh! Grav - i - ty. ___ Why _ can't we ___ seem to

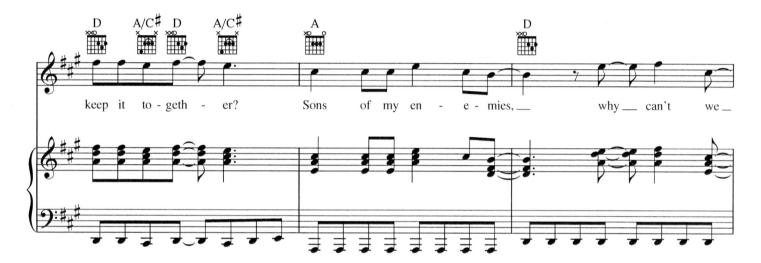

keep it to - geth - er? Sons of my en - e - mies, ___ why ___ can't we _

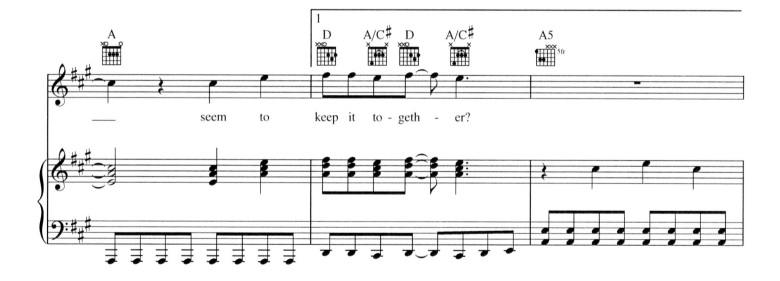

___ seem to keep it to - geth - er?

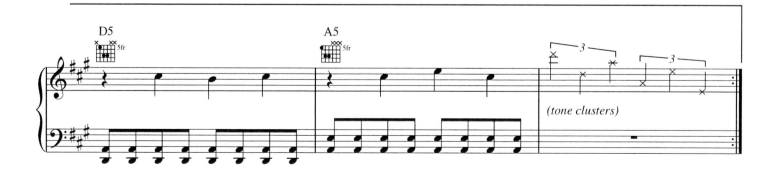

(tone clusters)

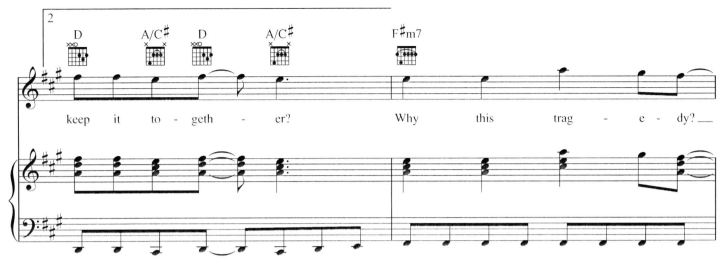

keep it to - geth - er? Why this trag - e - dy?___

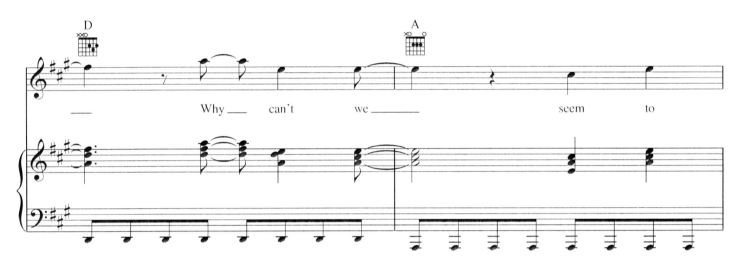

___ Why___ can't we_____ seem to

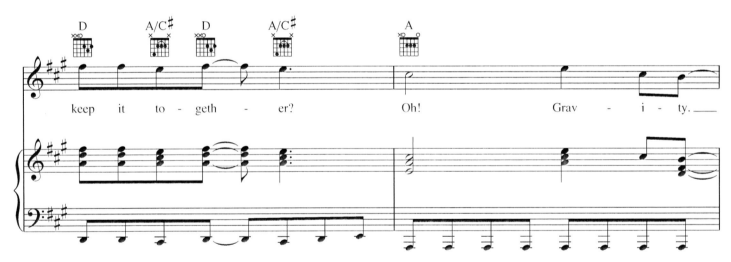

keep it to - geth - er? Oh! Grav - i - ty.___

___ Why__ can't we___ seem to pull it to - geth - er?

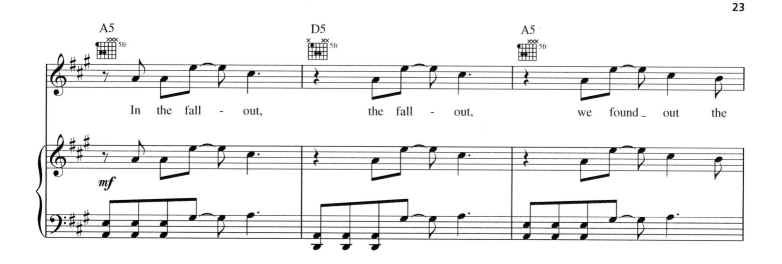

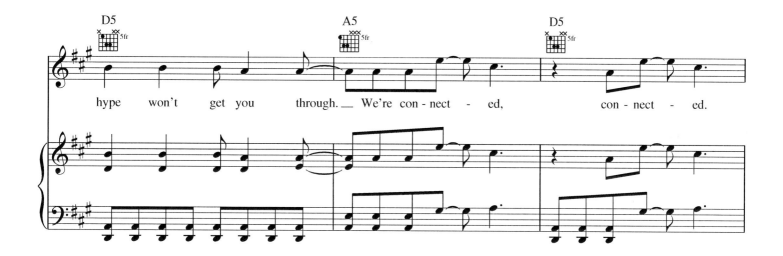

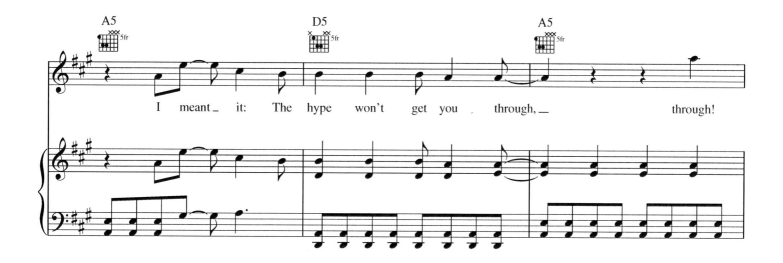

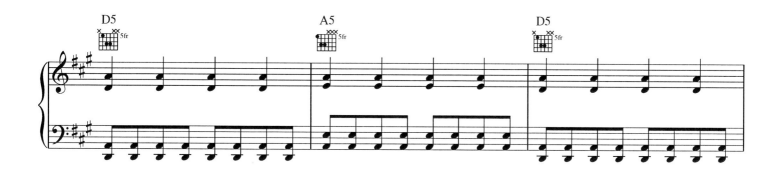

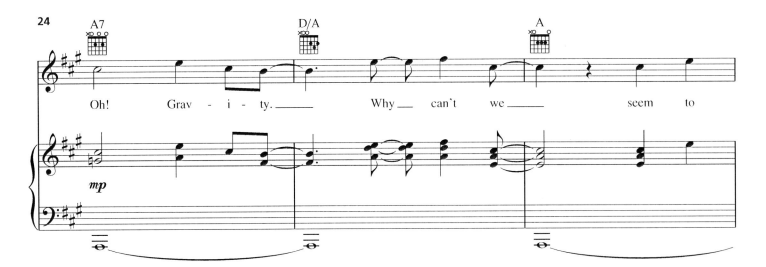

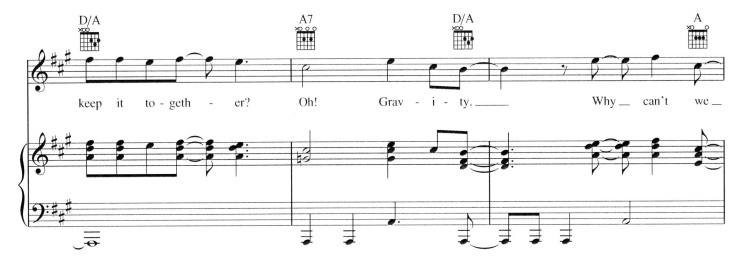

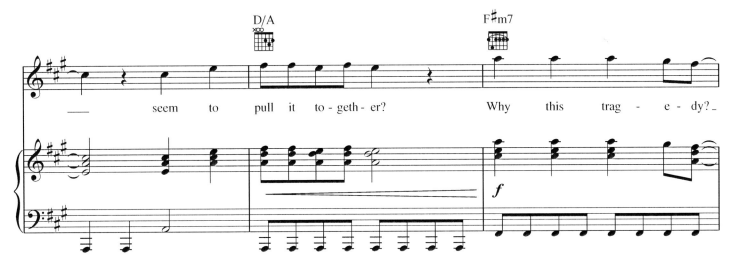

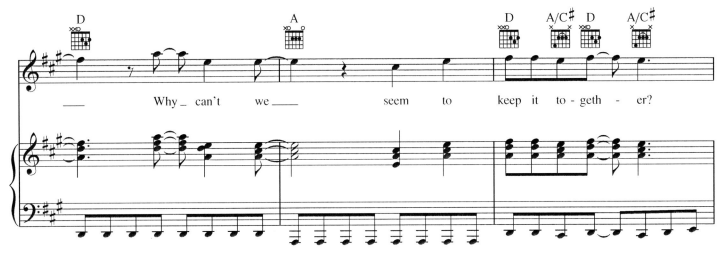

Oh! Grav - i - ty. ___ Why ___ can't we ___ seem to

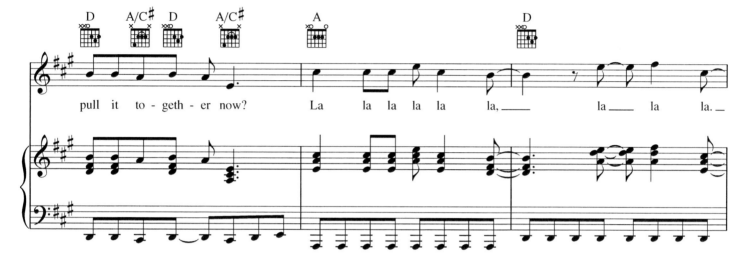

pull it to - geth - er now? La la la la la la, ___ la ___ la la. ___

___ La la la la la la ___ la. La ___ la la la la la, ___

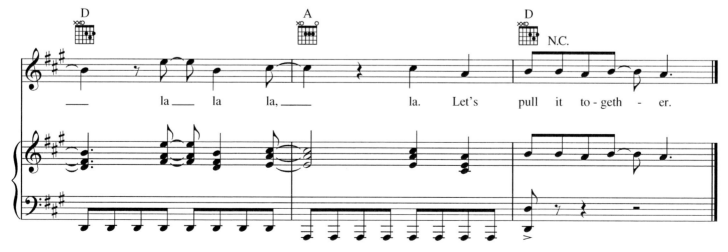

___ la ___ la la, ___ la. Let's pull it to - geth - er.

STARS

Words and Music by
JONATHAN FOREMAN

Driving Rock

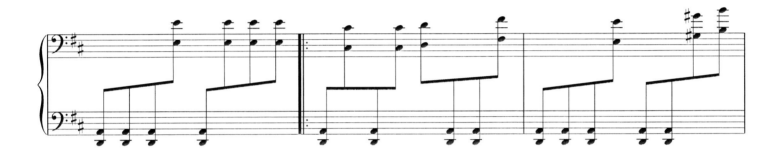

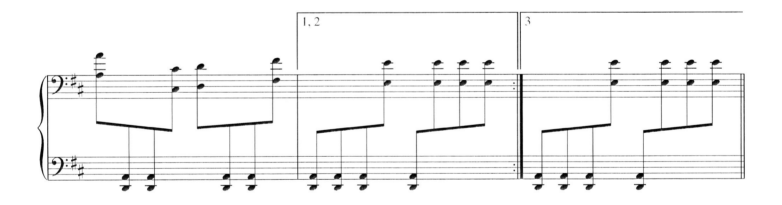

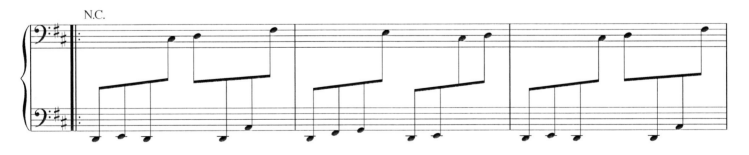

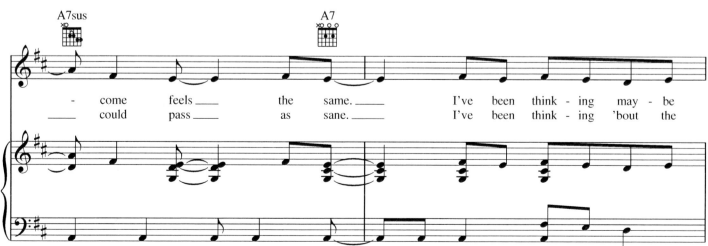

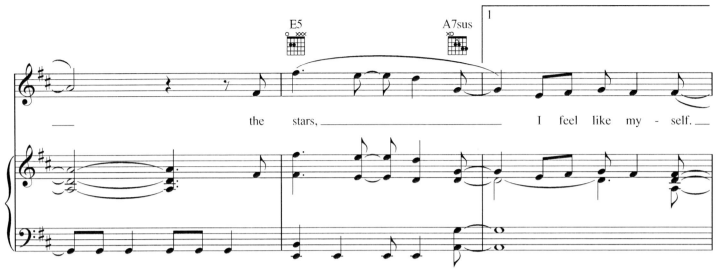

the stars, _____ I feel like my - self. __

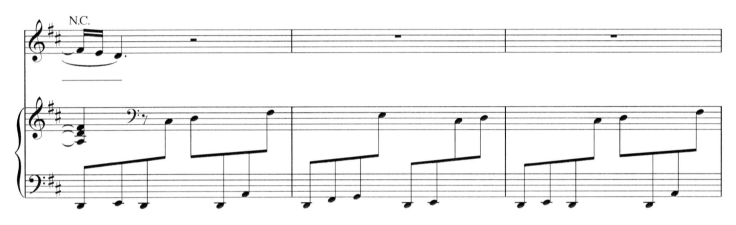

I feel like my - self. _____ Yeah!

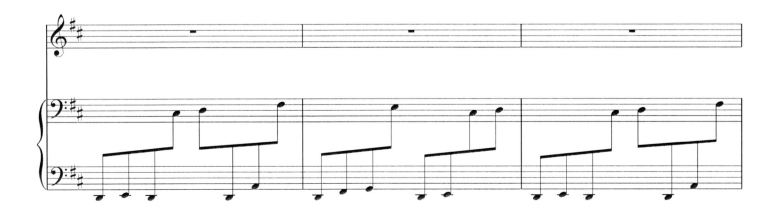

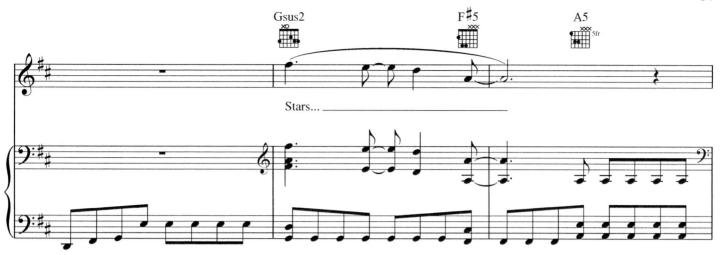

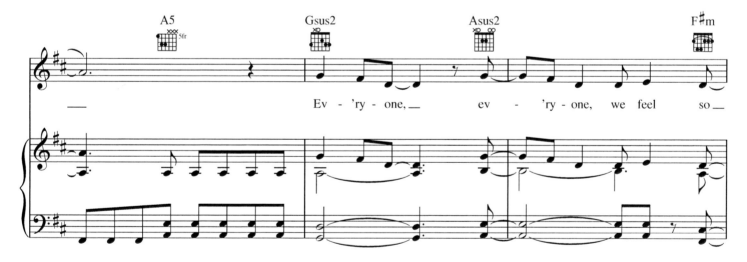

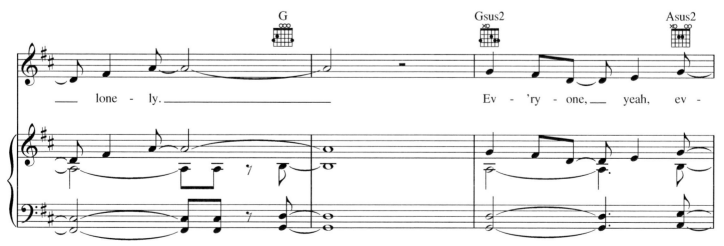

the   stars, _____ I   see   some - one.

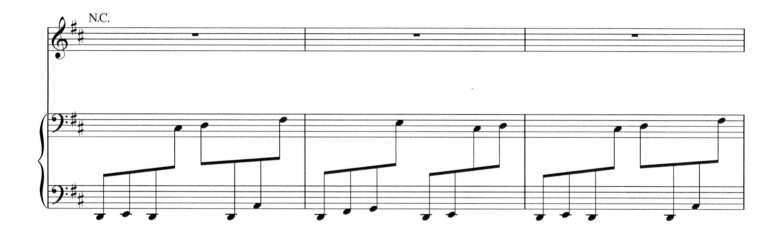

THIS IS HOME

from Walt Disney Pictures' and Walden Media's
THE CHRONICLES OF NARNIA: PRINCE CASPIAN

Written by JONATHAN FOREMAN,
ANDY DODD and ADAM WATTS

I've got my mem-o-ries al-

-ways in-side of me, but I can't go back,

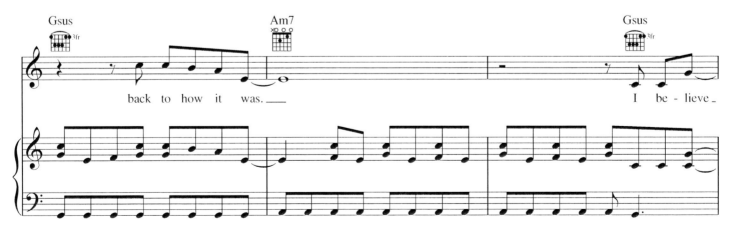

back to how it was. I be-lieve

you now; _____ I've come ___ too far.

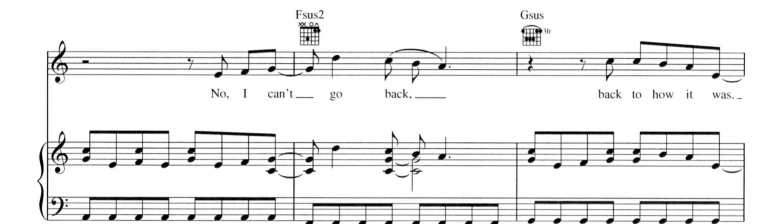

No, I can't ___ go back, _____ back to how it was. _

_____ Cre - at - ed for ___ a place _

_____ I've nev - er known, _____ this is home. _

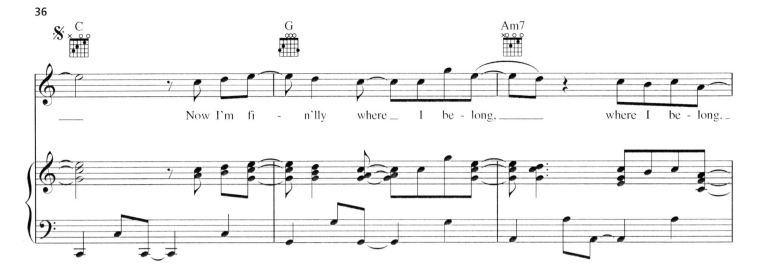

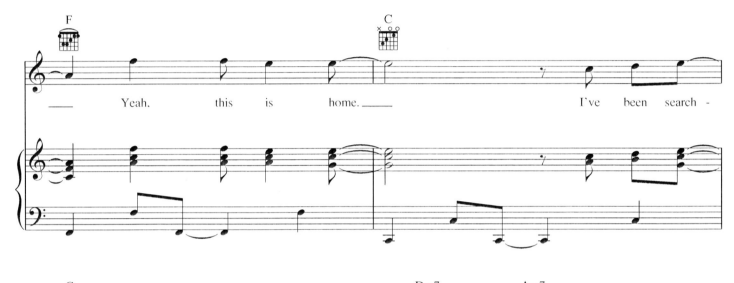

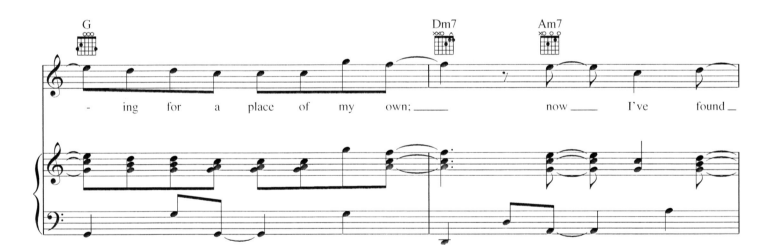

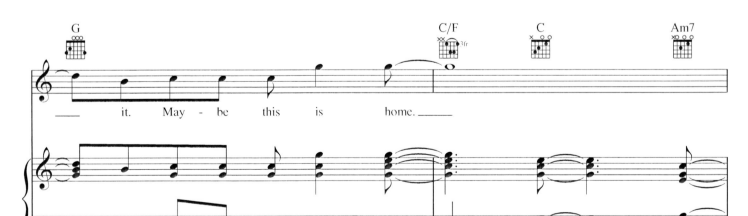

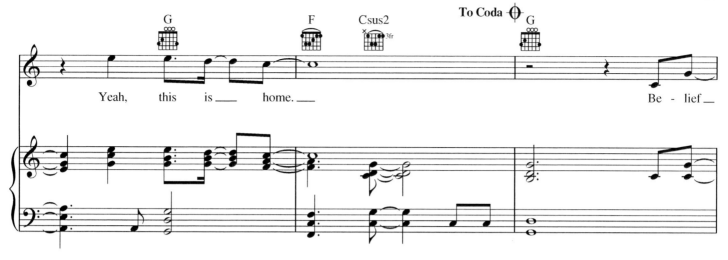

Yeah, this is ___ home. ___ Be - lief ___

___ o - ver mis - er - y, ___ I've ___ seen the en - e - my, ___

___ and I won't ___ go back, ___ back to how it was. _

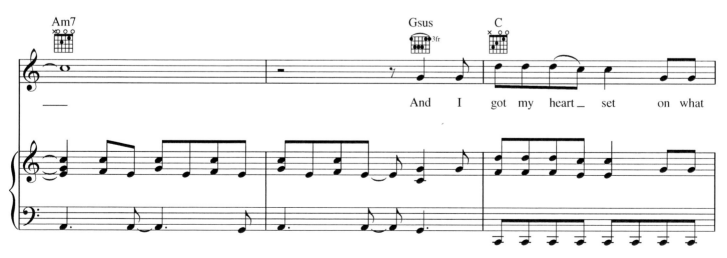

___ And I got my heart ___ set on what

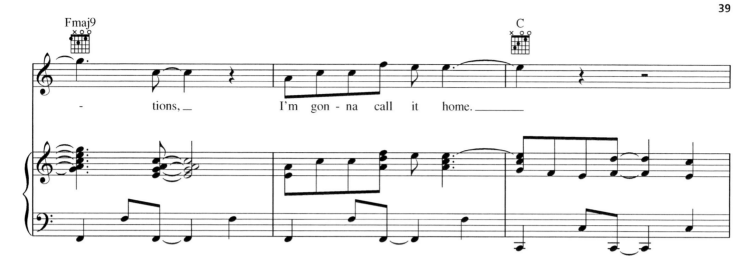

- tions, __ I'm gon - na call it home. _____

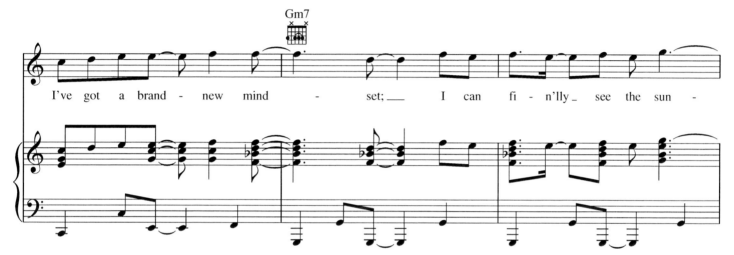

I've got a brand - new mind - set; __ I can fi - n'lly _ see the sun -

- set. __ I'm gon - na call it home. _____

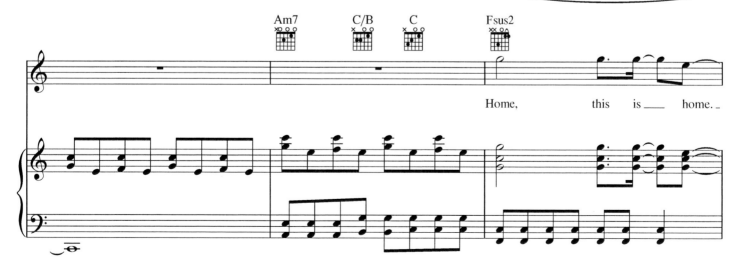

Home, this is __ home. _

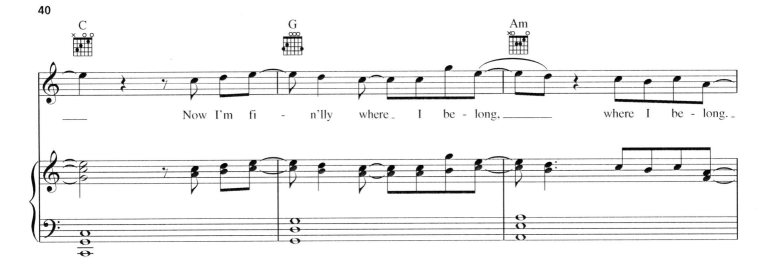

Now I'm fi - n'lly where I be - long, _____ where I be - long. _

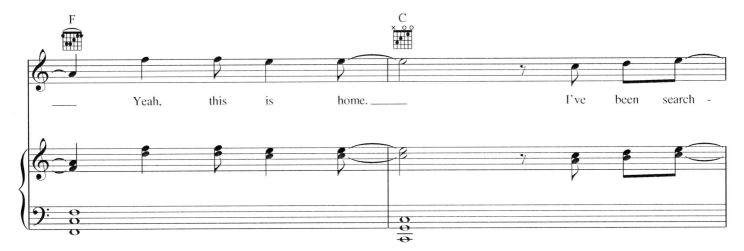

_ Yeah, this is home. _____ I've been search -

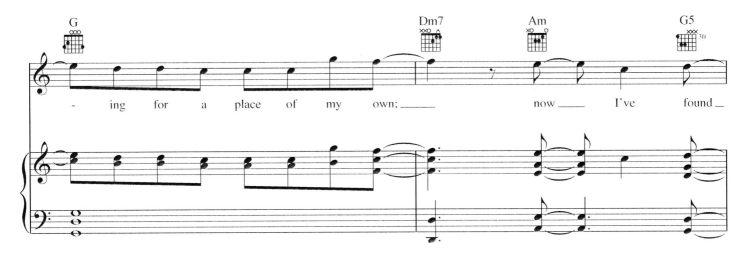

- ing for a place of my own; _____ now _____ I've found _

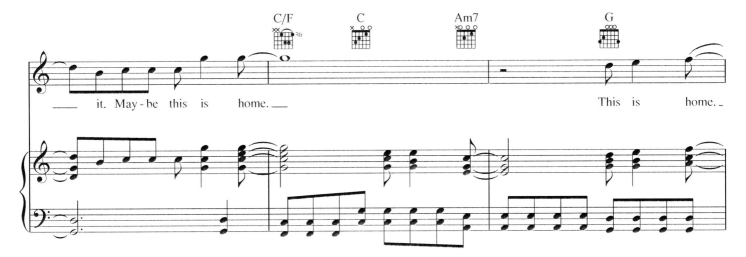

_____ it. May - be this is home. ___ This is home. _

LEARNING TO BREATHE

Words and Music by
JONATHAN FOREMAN

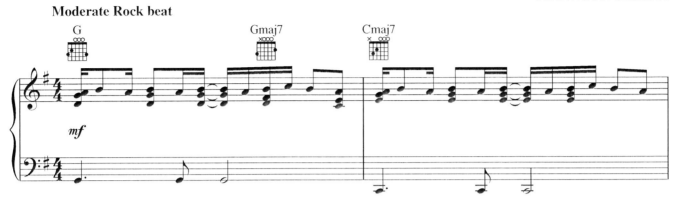

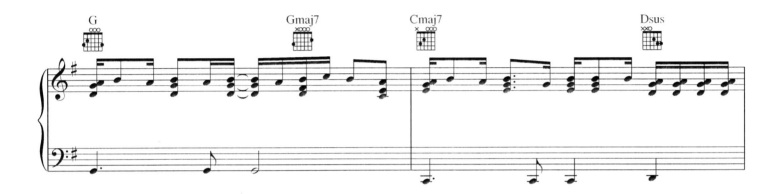

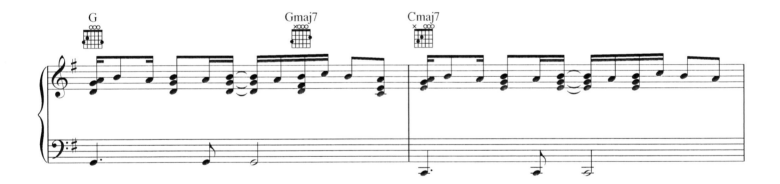

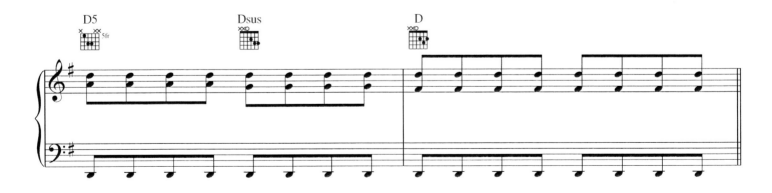

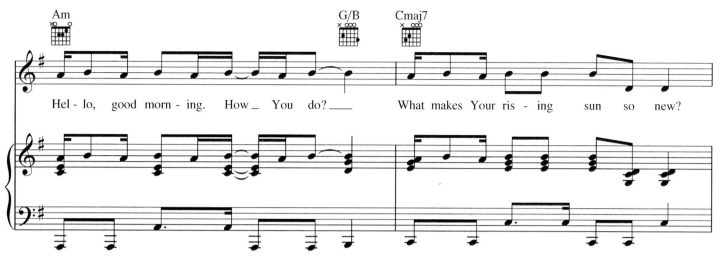

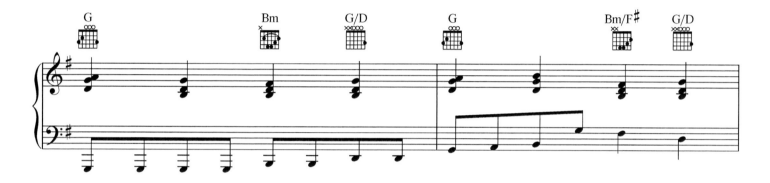

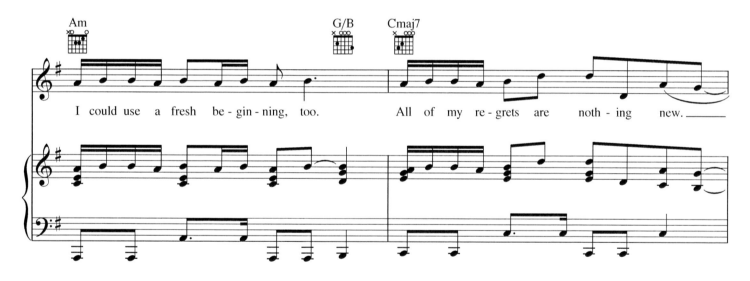

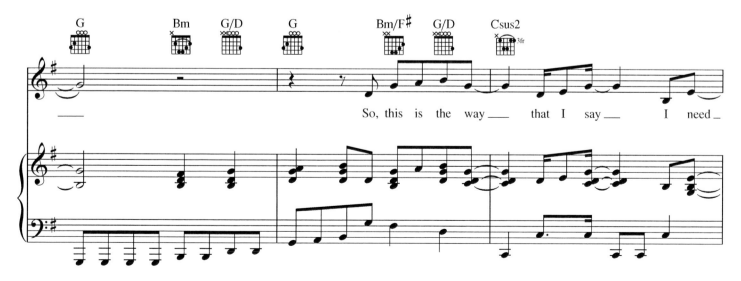

You. This is the way, ___ this is the way ___ that I'm learn - ing to breathe, ___

I'm learn - ing to crawl, ___ I'm find - ing that You ___

and You a - lone ___ can break ___ my fall. I'm liv - ing a - gain, ___

a - wake and a - live. ___ I'm dy - ing to breathe ___

D.S. al Coda

I'm learn - ing to breathe, _

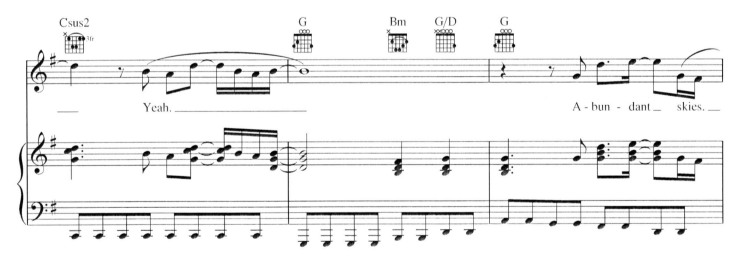

These a - bun - dant skies. _

Yeah. _

A - bun - dant _ skies. _

Yeah. _

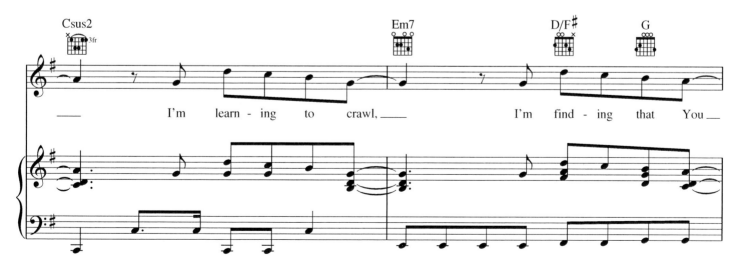

___ and You a - lone__ can break__ my fall._ _I'm liv - ing a - gain,___

___ a - wake and a - live.___ _I'm dy - ing to breathe ___

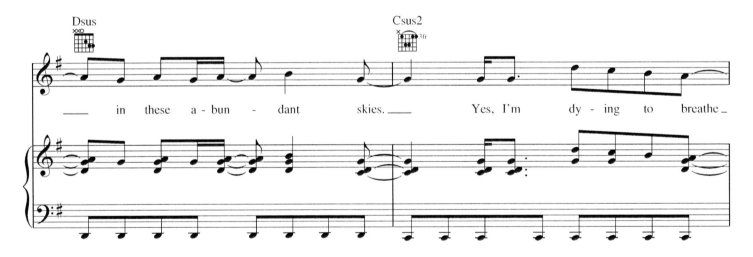

___ in these a - bun - dant skies. ___ _Yes, I'm dy - ing to breathe ___

___ in these a - bun - dant skies, ___ _these a - bun - dant skies. ___

50

in these a - bun - dant skies. Hel - lo, good morn - ing. How_ You do?_

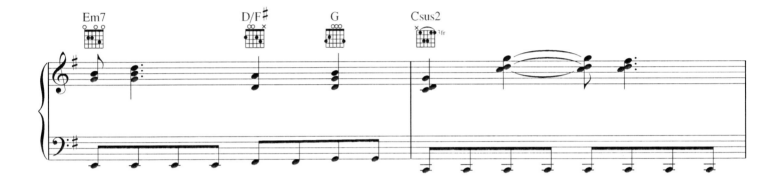

THIS IS YOUR LIFE

Words and Music by
JONATHAN FOREMAN

Moderately slow, in 2

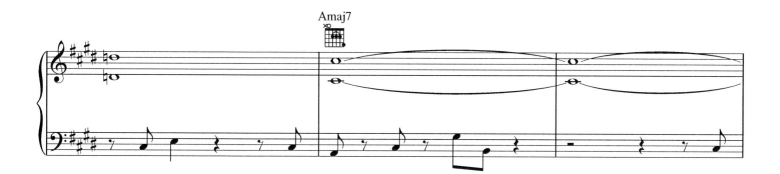

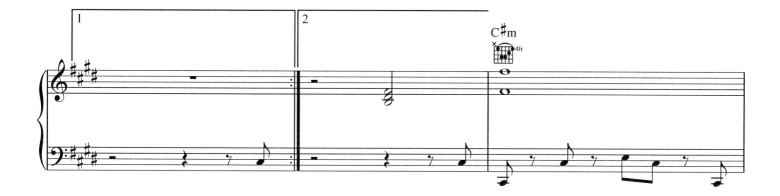

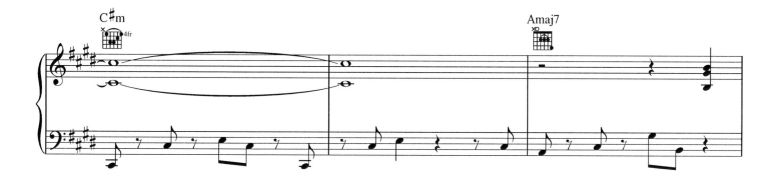

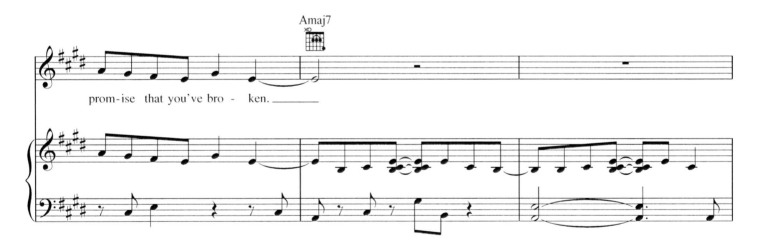

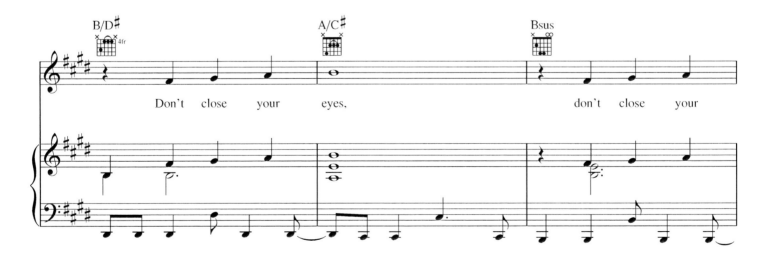

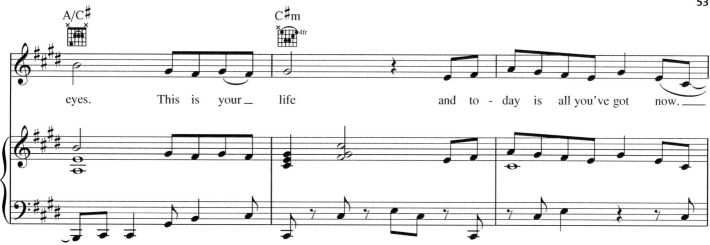

eyes. This is your _ life and to-day is all you've got now. _

And, and to-

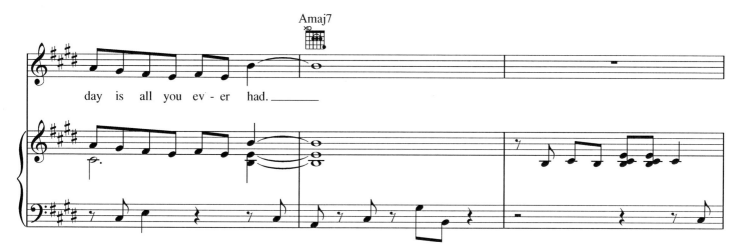

day is all you ev-er had. _

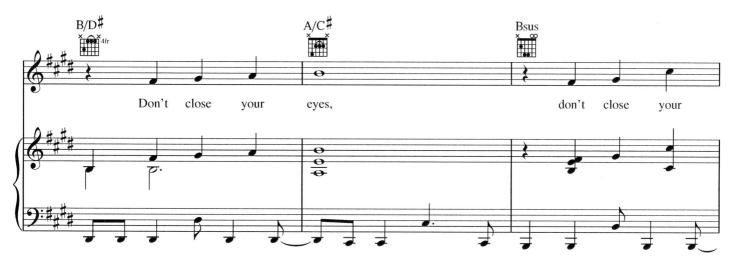

Don't close your eyes, don't close your

eyes. This is your __ life; are you who __ you want __ to be? __

__ This is your __ life; are you who __

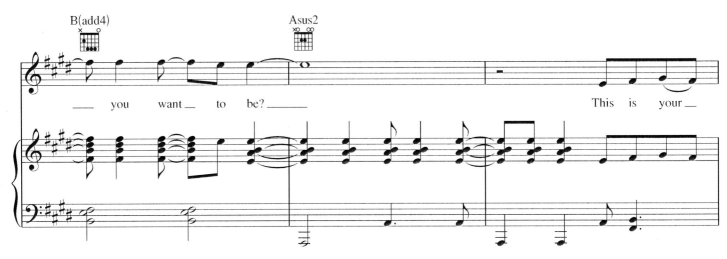

__ you want __ to be? __ This is your __

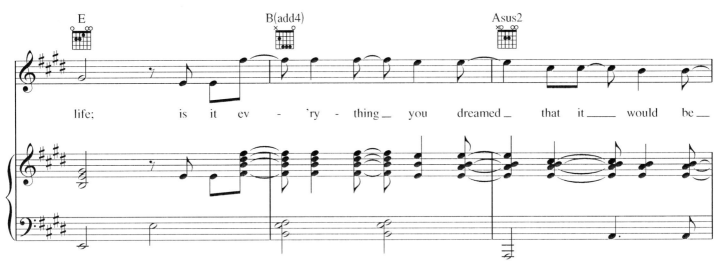

life; is it ev - 'ry - thing __ you dreamed __ that it __ would be __

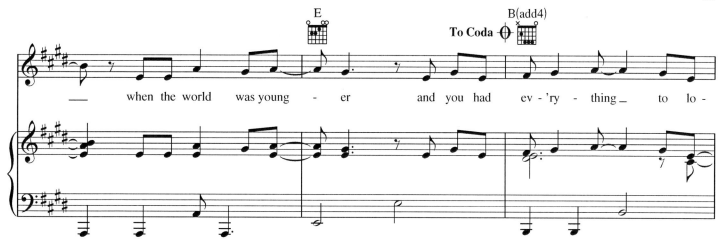

when the world was young - er and you had ev-'ry-thing __ to lo -

- o - o - o - ose?

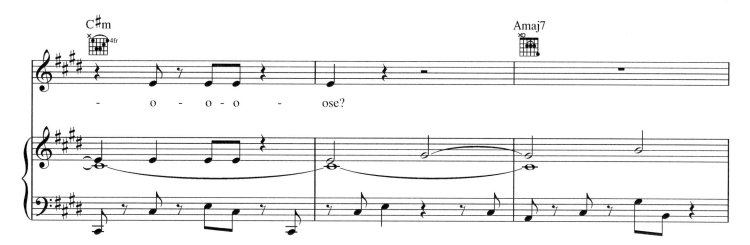

Yes - ter - day is a kid in the cor - ner. ____

____ Yes - ter - day is

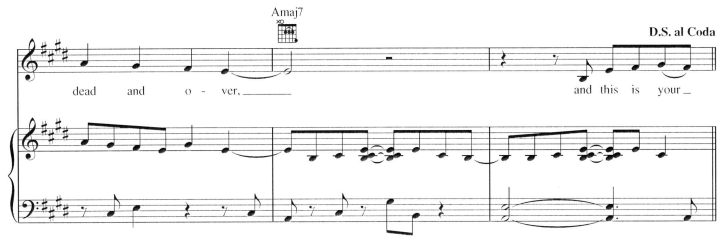

dead and o - ver, _____ and this is your _

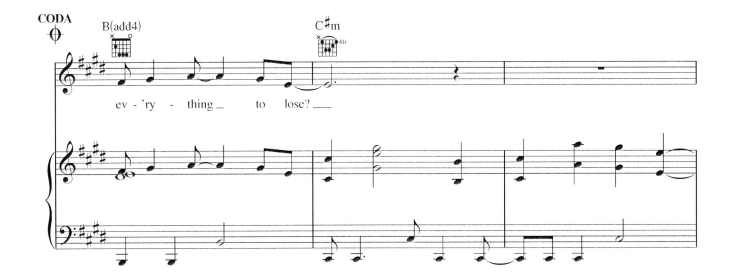

ev - 'ry - thing _ to lose? ___

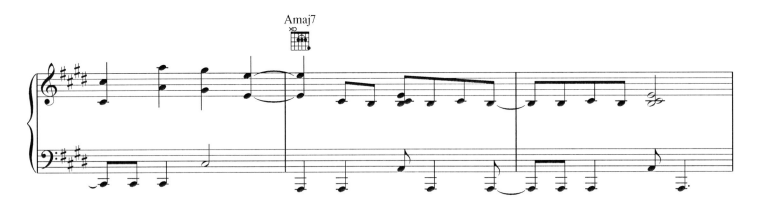

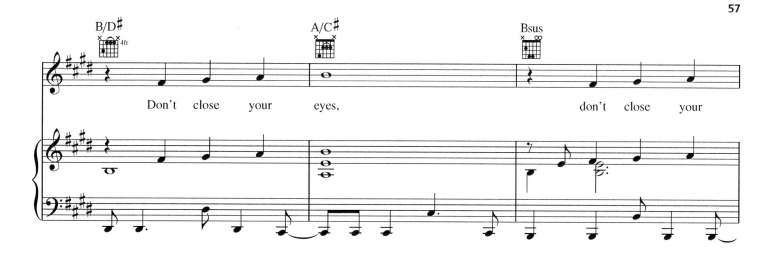

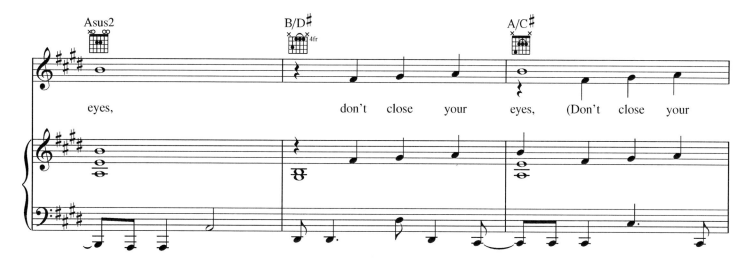

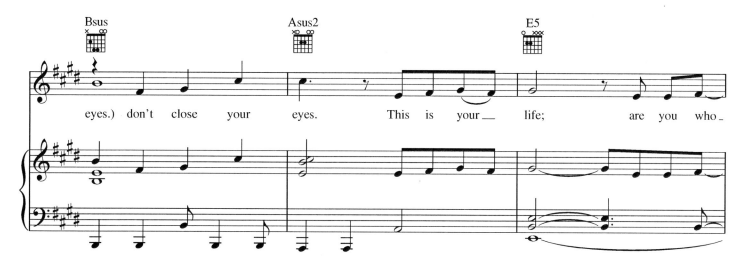

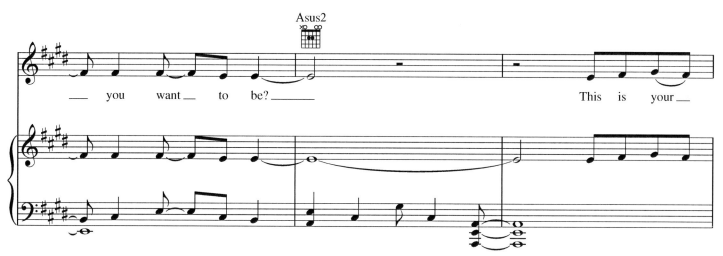

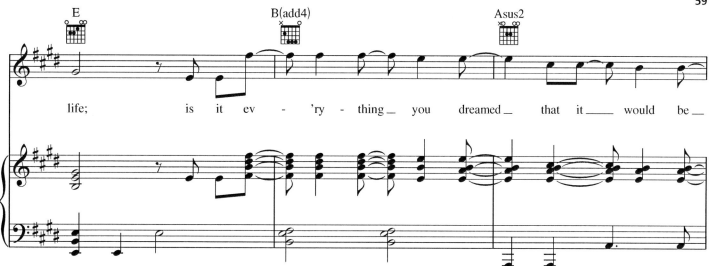

life; is it ev - 'ry - thing — you dreamed — that it — would be —

— when the world was young - er and you had ev - 'ry - thing — to lose, —

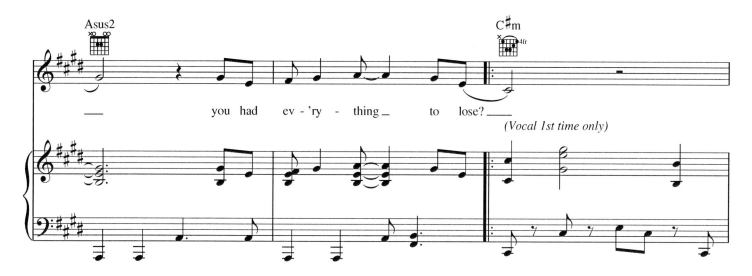

— you had ev - 'ry - thing — to lose? ——

(Vocal 1st time only)

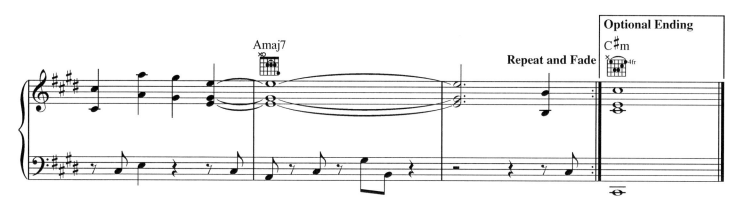

Repeat and Fade

Optional Ending

AWAKENING

Words and Music by
JONATHAN FOREMAN

Driving Rock beat

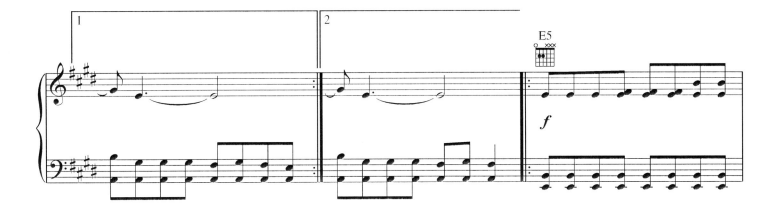

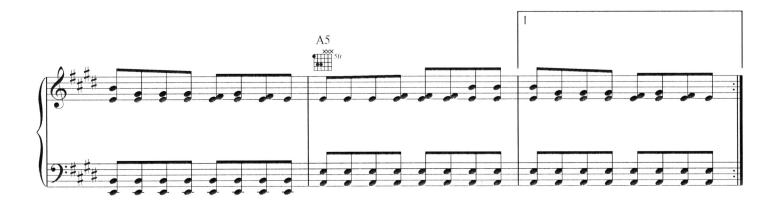

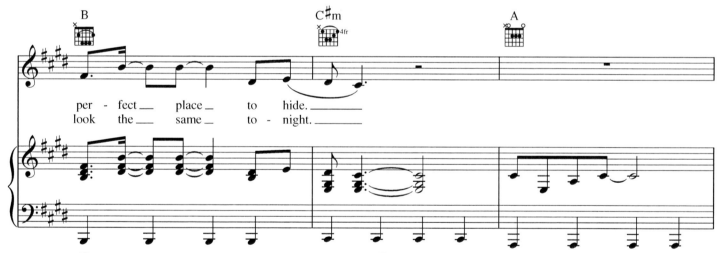

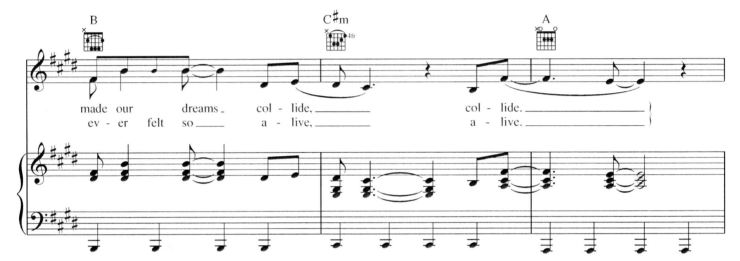

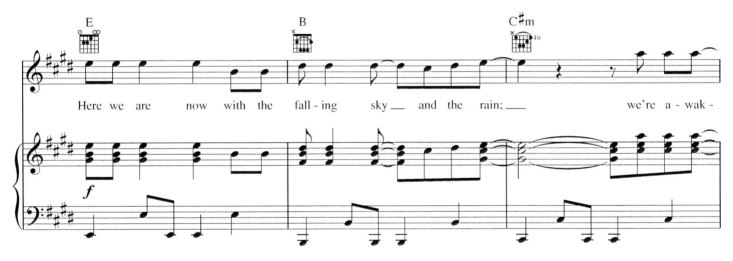

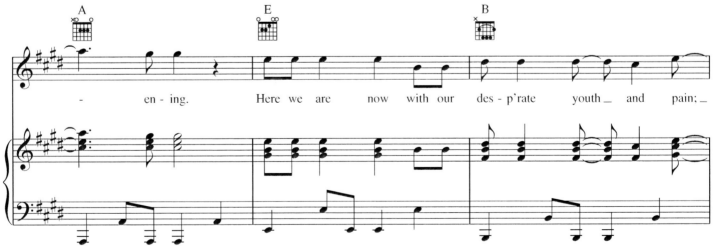

we're a-wak - en - ing. May-be it's called_ am - bi -

- tion; you've been talk-ing in_ your sleep_ a-bout a dream._

We're a-wak - en - ing.

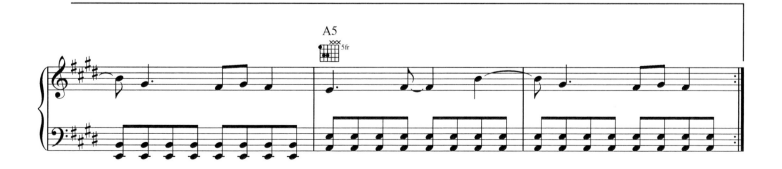

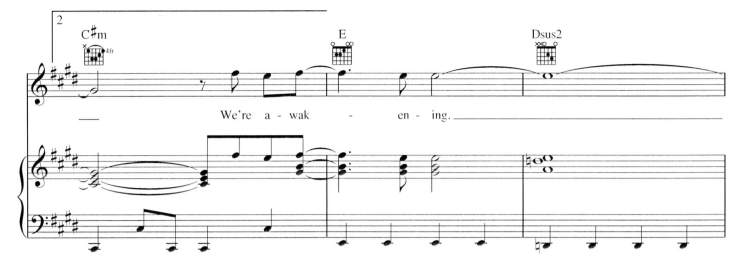

We're a - wak - en - ing.

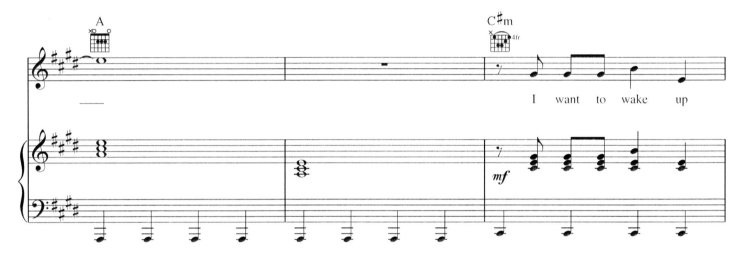

I want to wake up

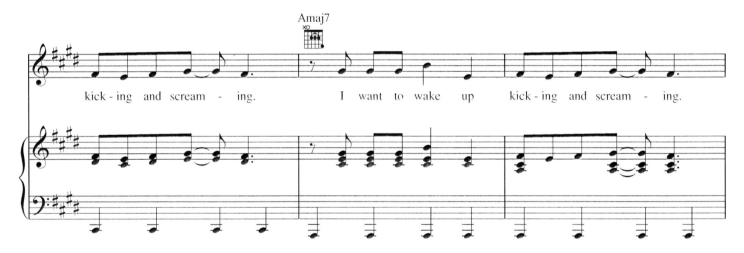

kick - ing and scream - ing. I want to wake up kick - ing and scream - ing.

I want to know that my heart's still __ beat - ing. It's beat - ing,

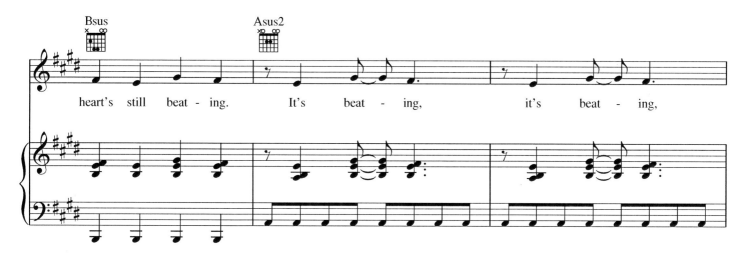

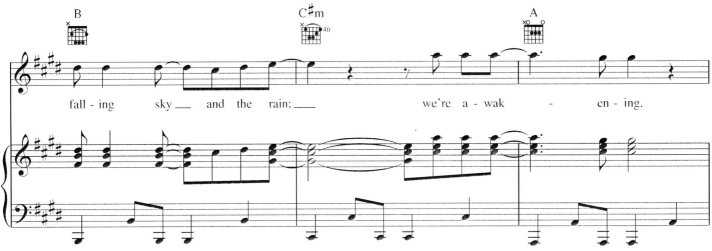

fall - ing sky __ and the rain; __ we're a - wak - en - ing.

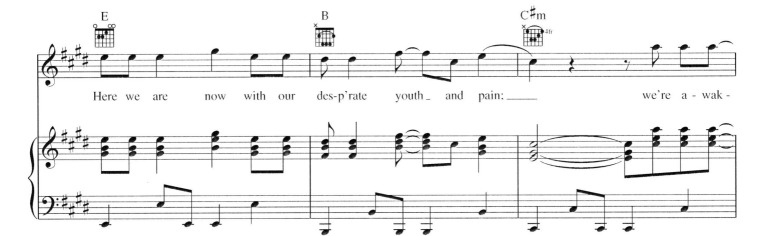

Here we are now with our des-p'rate youth __ and pain; __ we're a - wak -

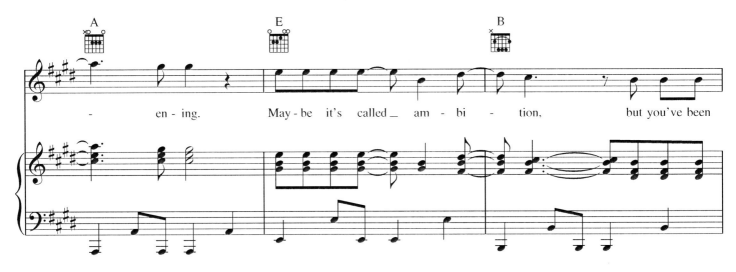

- en - ing. May - be it's called __ am - bi - tion, but you've been

talk, talk - ing in your sleep __ a - bout a dream. __ We're a - wak -

-en - ing. Dream, ___ we're a - wak - en - ing, yeah!

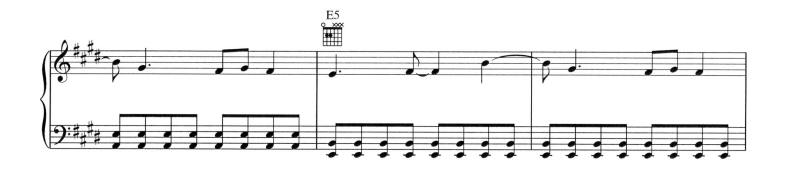

ON FIRE

Words and Music by JONATHAN FOREMAN
and DANIEL VICTOR

Moderately slow

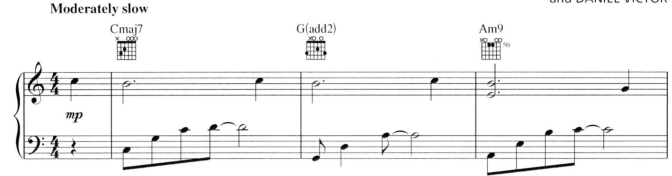

They tell you where __ you need __ to go, __

__ they tell you when __ you need ___ to leave. ___

They tell you what __ you need __ to know, __

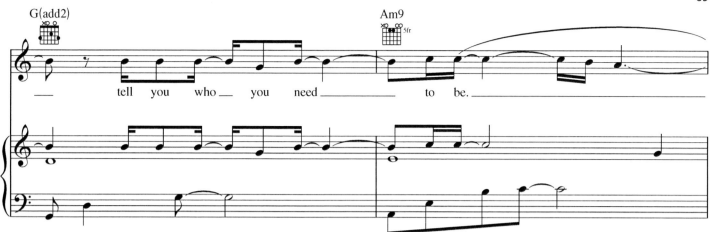

tell you who _ you need _____ to be. ____

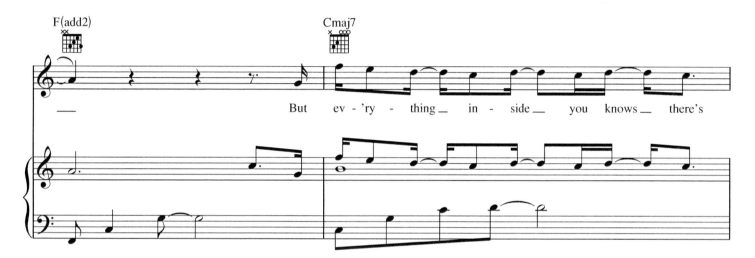

__ But ev - 'ry - thing _ in - side _ you knows _ there's

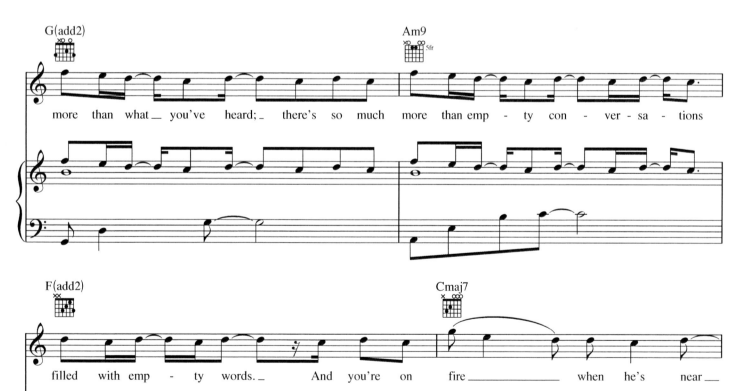

more than what _ you've heard; _ there's so much more than emp - ty con - ver - sa - tions

filled with emp - ty words. _ And you're on fire _____ when he's near __

you, you're on fire _____ when he speaks. _____ You're on fire, _____

_____ burn - ing at these mys - ter - ies. _____

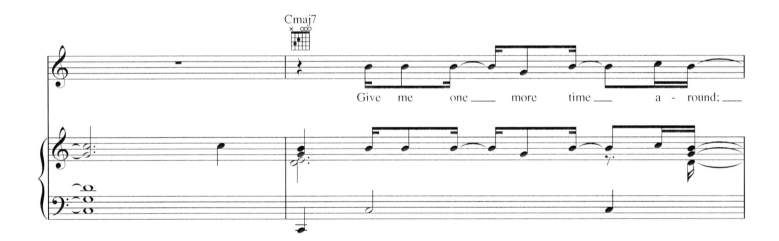

Give me one ____ more time ____ a - round; ____

____ give me one ____ more chance _____ to see. _____

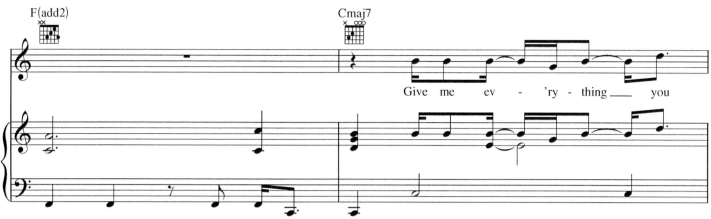

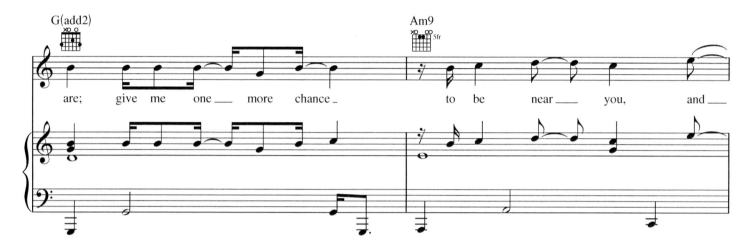

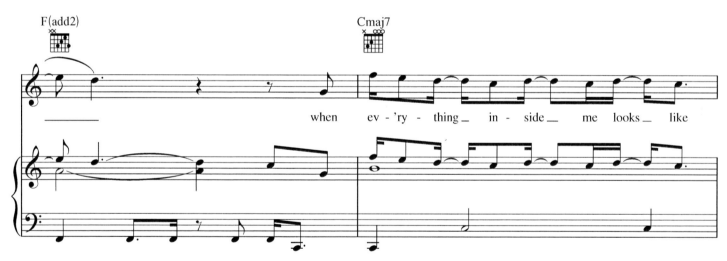

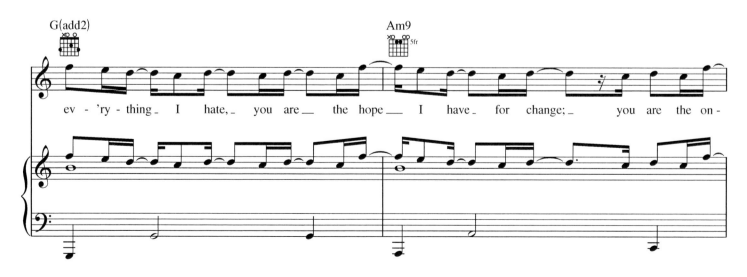

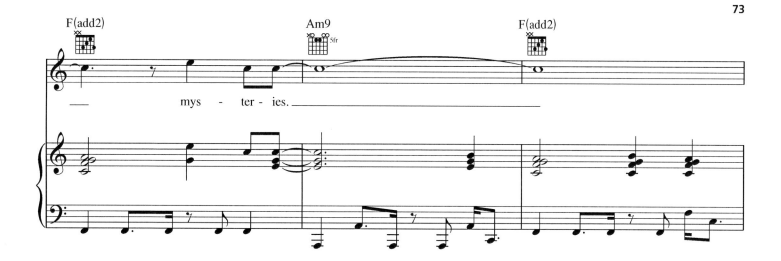

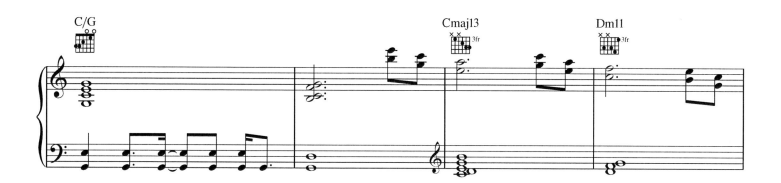

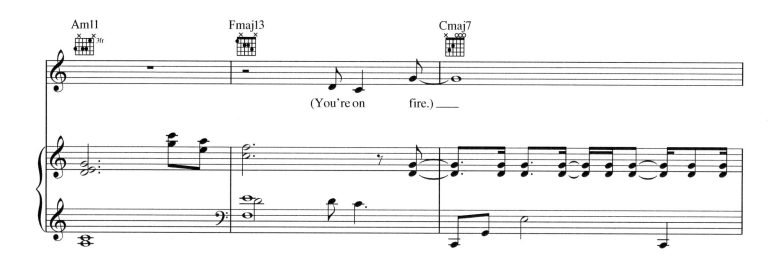

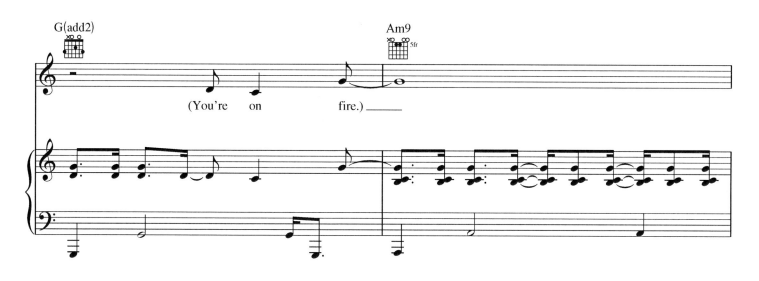

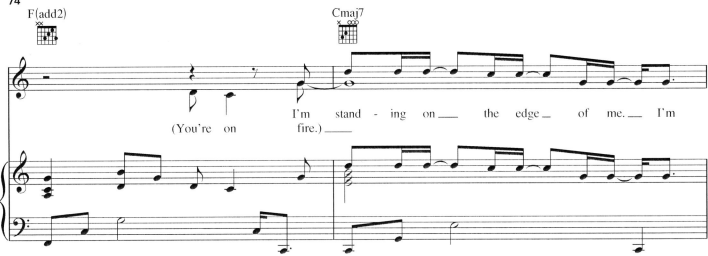

I'm stand-ing on ___ the edge ___ of me. ___ I'm
(You're on fire.) ___

stand-ing on ___ the edge ___ of me. ___ I'm stand-ing on ___ the edge ___ of me. ___ I'm

stand-ing on ___ the edge ___ of me. ___ I'm stand-ing on ___ the edge ___ of ev-'ry-thing ___

___ I've nev-er been be-fore, and I've been stand-ing on ___ the edge ___ of me, ___

stand - ing on __ the edge. __ And I'm __ on fire _____ when you're near __

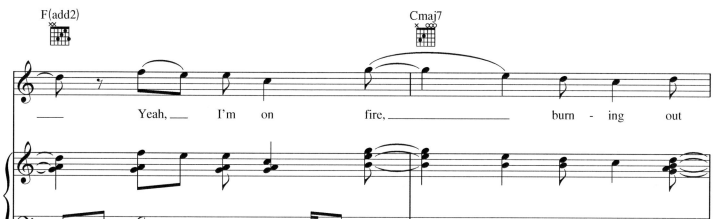

__ me. I'm on fire _____ when you speak. __

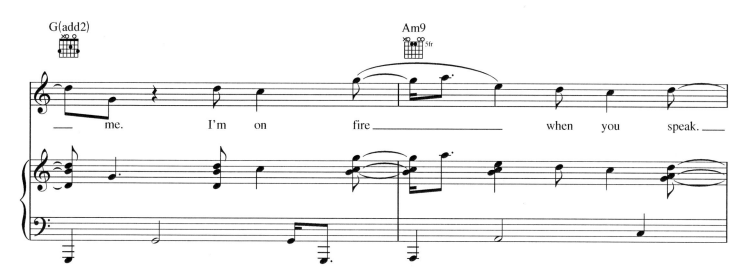

__ Yeah, __ I'm on fire, _____ burn - ing out

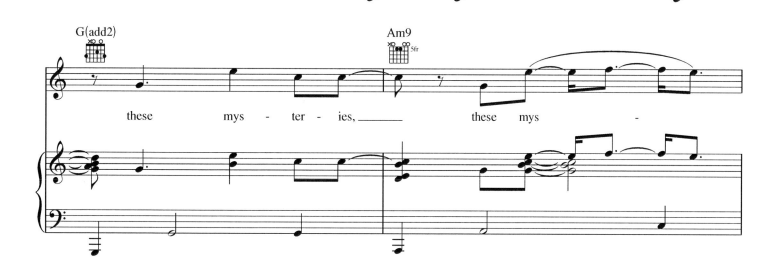

these mys - ter - ies, _____ these mys -

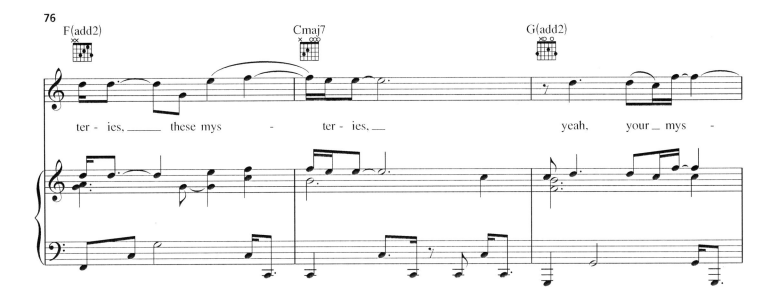

ter - ies, _____ these mys - ter - ies, _____ yeah, your _ mys -

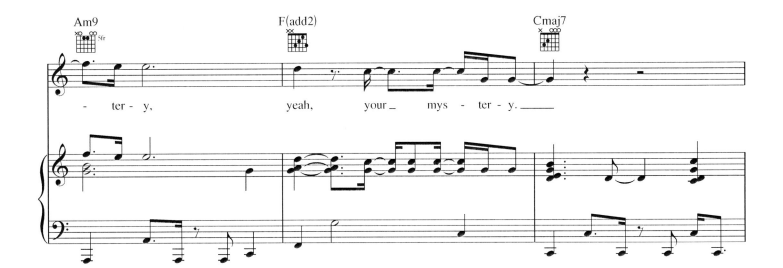

- ter - y, yeah, your _ mys - ter - y. _____

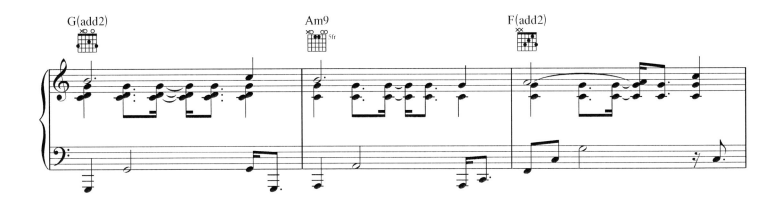

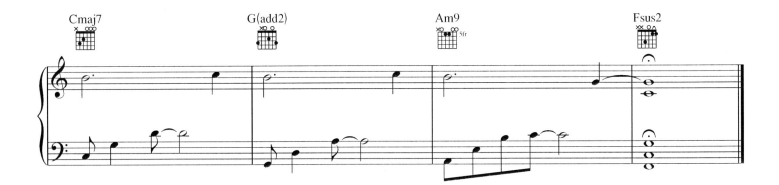

ONLY HOPE

from the Warner Bros. Motion Picture A WALK TO REMEMBER

Words and Music by
JONATHAN FOREMAN

Fast Waltz, in 1

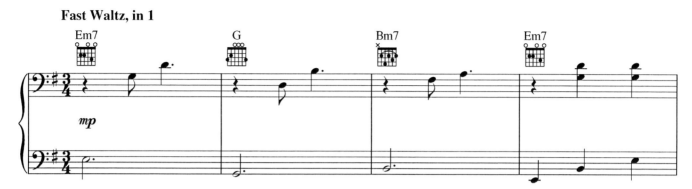

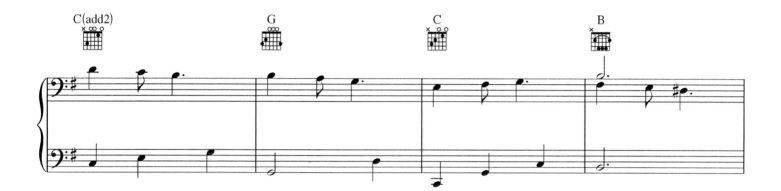

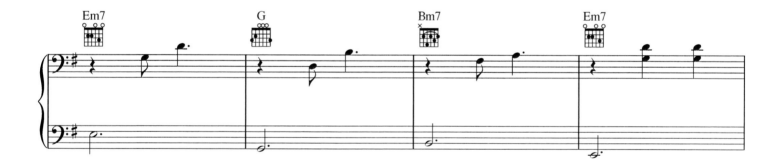

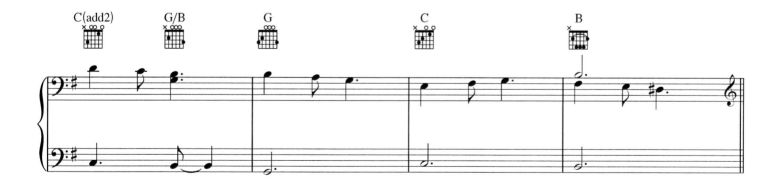

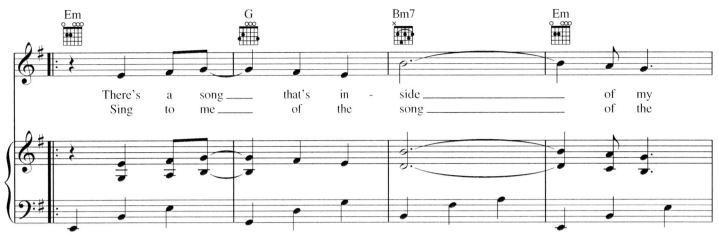

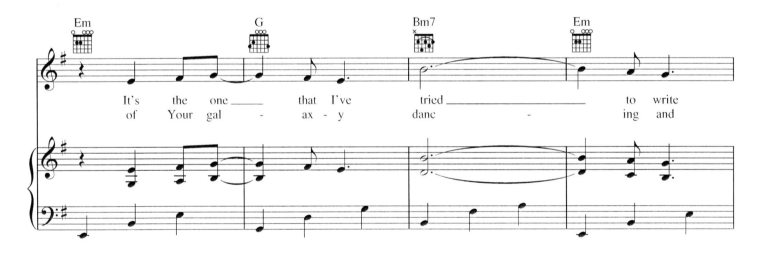

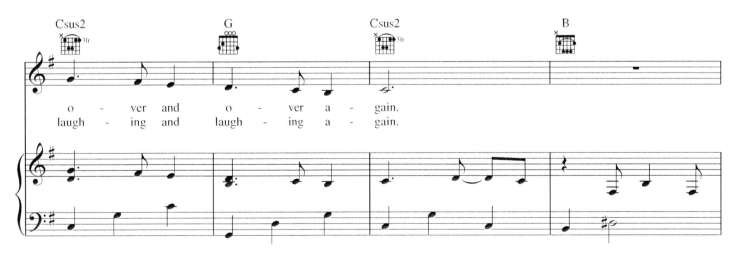

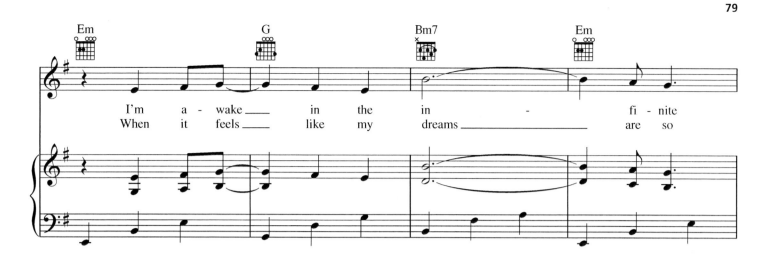

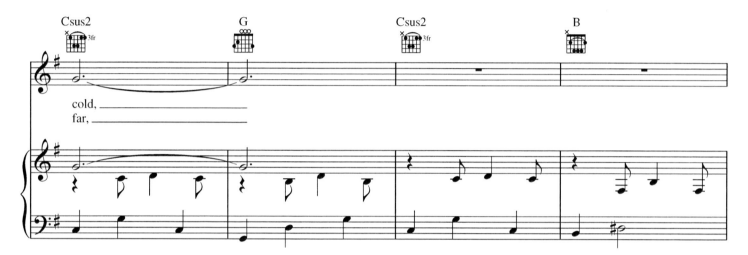

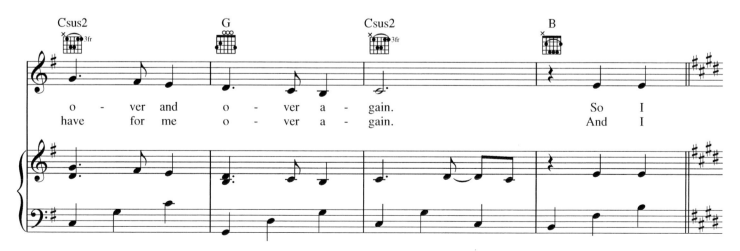

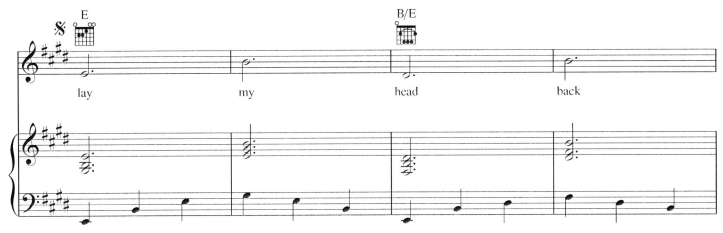

lay   my   head   back

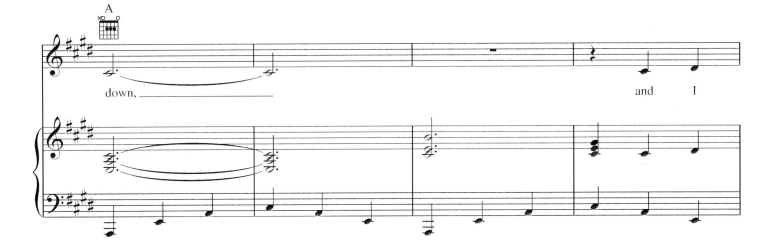

down, _____   and   I

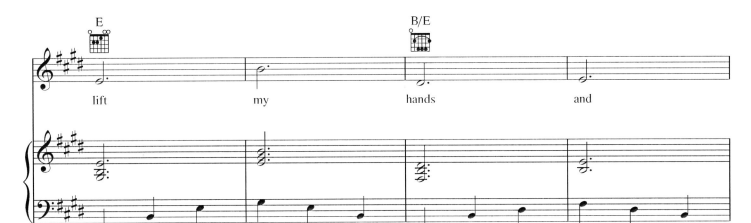

lift   my   hands   and

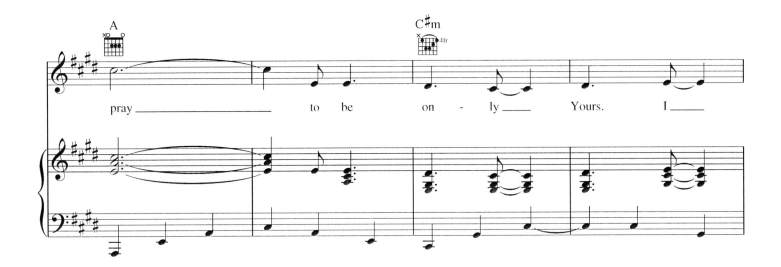

pray _____   to   be   on - ly ____ Yours.   I ____

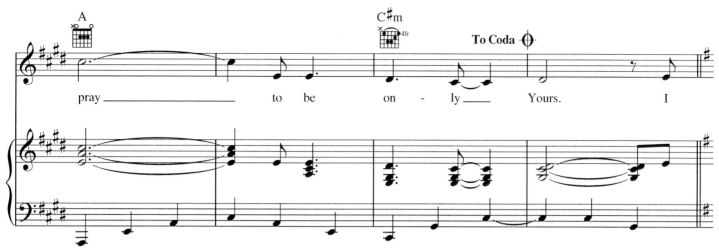

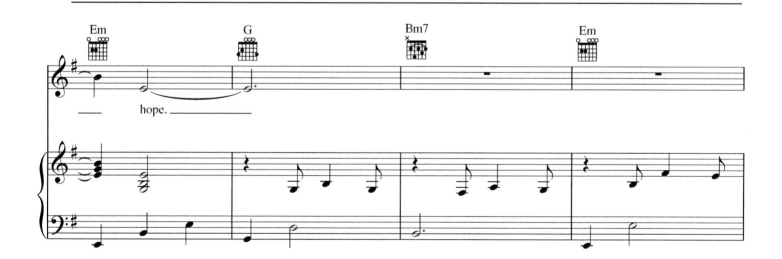

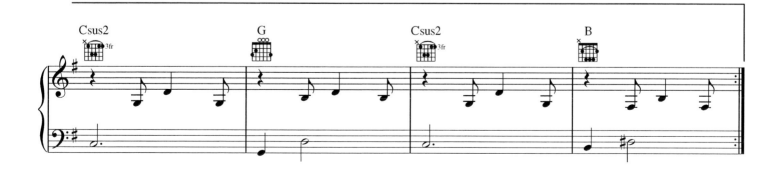

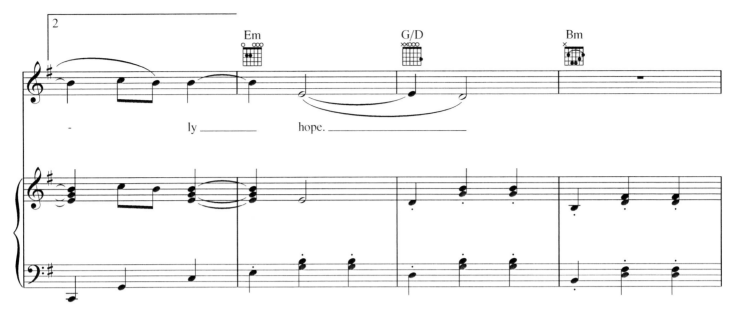

ly _____ hope. _____

simile

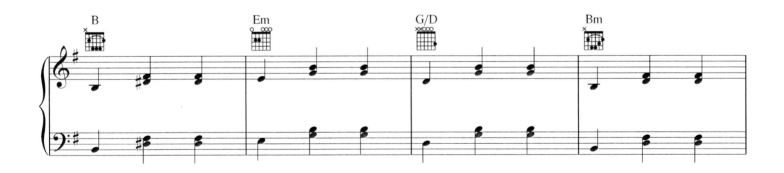

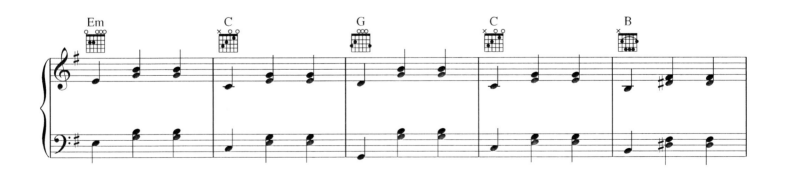

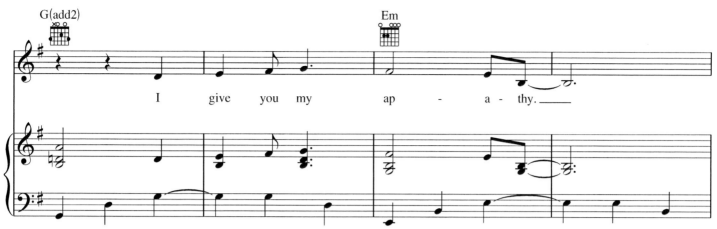

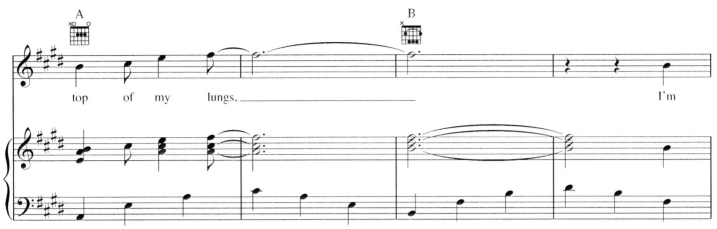

top of my lungs,_____ I'm

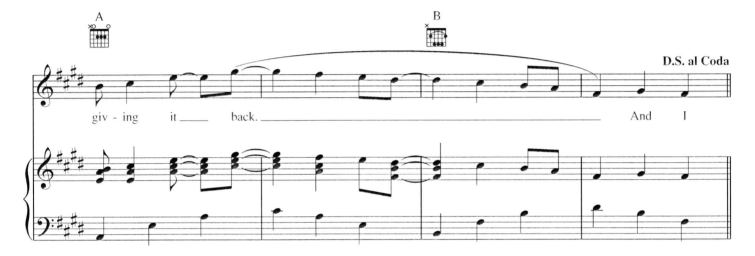

D.S. al Coda

giv - ing it___ back._____ And I

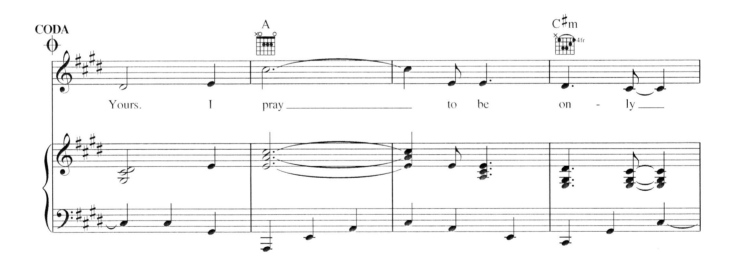

Yours. I pray_____ to be on - ly___

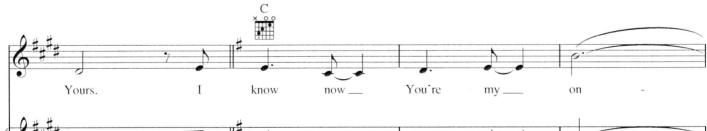

Yours. I know now___ You're my___ on -

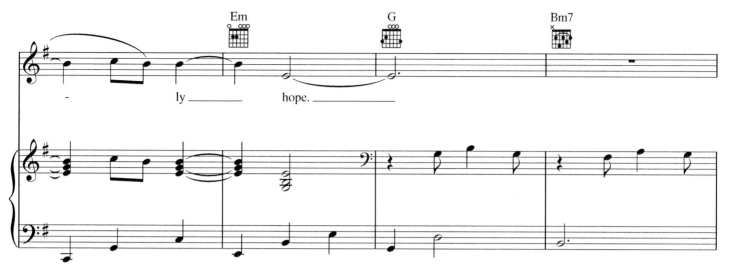

ly _____ hope. _____

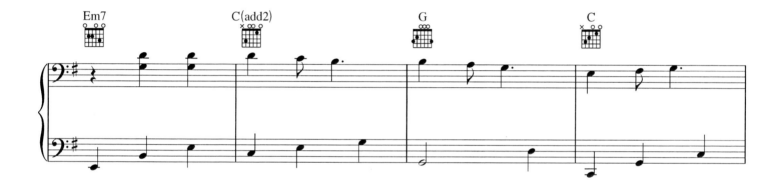

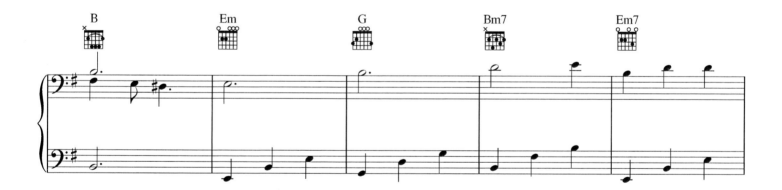

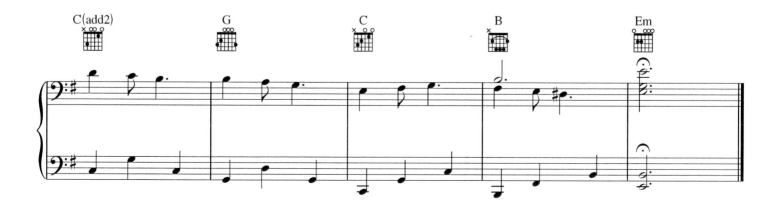

DIRTY SECOND HANDS

Words and Music by JONATHAN FOREMAN
and TODD COOPER

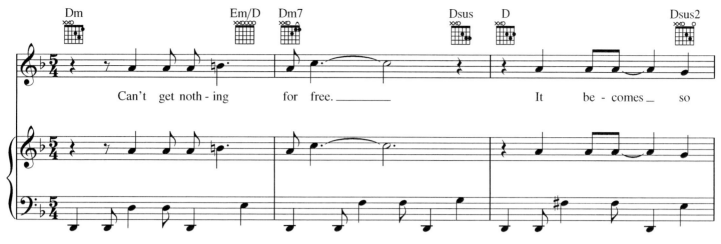

Can't get noth-ing for free. _____ It be-comes_ so

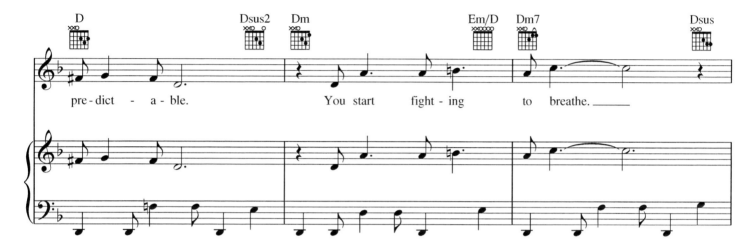

pre-dict-a-ble. You start fight-ing to breathe. _____

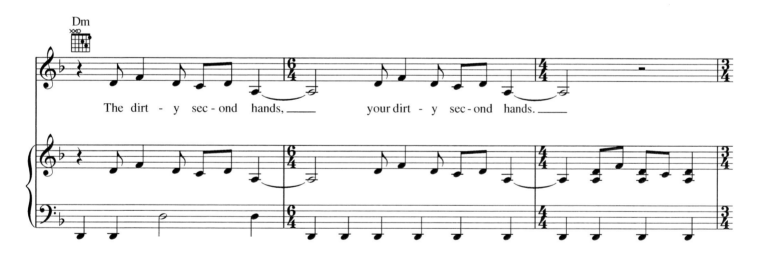

The dirt-y sec-ond hands, _____ your dirt-y sec-ond hands. _____

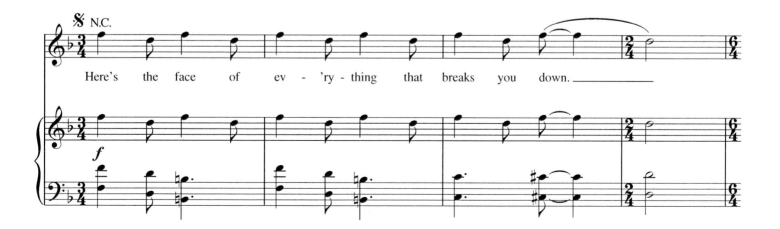

Here's the face of ev-'ry-thing that breaks you down. _____

But now you face the

face of ev - 'ry - thing that breaks you down. _____

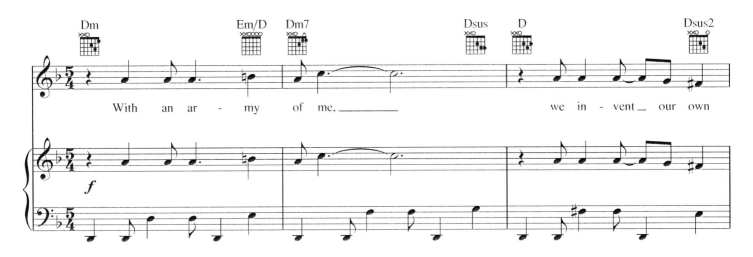

With an ar - my of me, _____ we in - vent _ our own

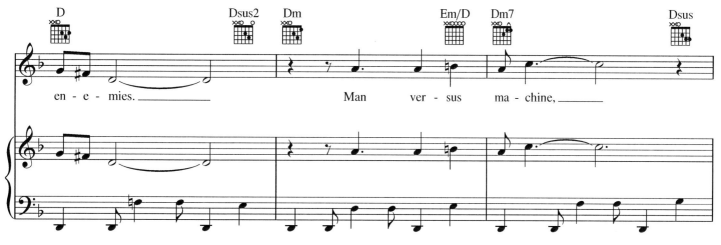

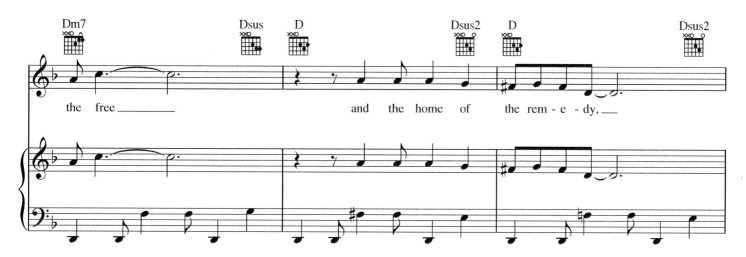

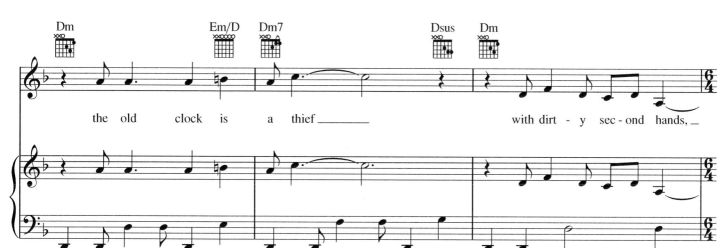

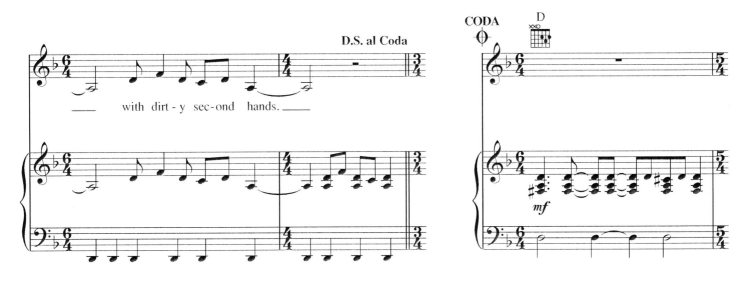

with dirt-y sec-ond hands.

You might be right;— the fight might be right in-side you, the blind lead-

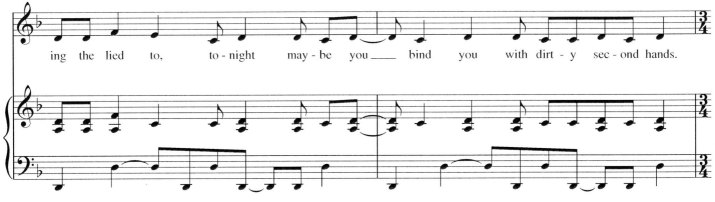

ing the lied to, to-night may-be you___ bind you with dirt-y sec-ond hands.

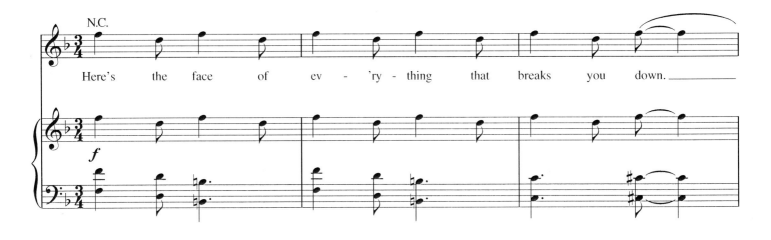

N.C.

Here's the face of ev-'ry-thing that breaks you down.___

Dm

N.C.

___ You bind you___ with dirt-y sec-ond hands. Now you face the

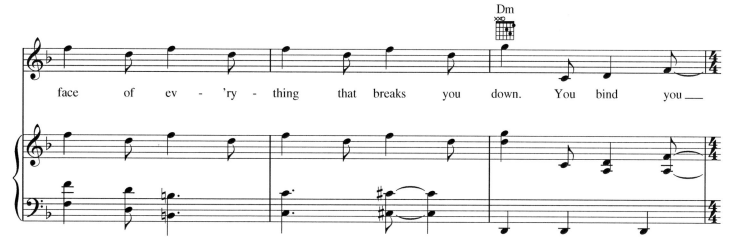

face of ev - 'ry - thing that breaks you down. You bind you ___

___ with dirt - y sec - ond hands. Now you face the

face of ev - 'ry - thing that breaks _ you down. ___

COMPANY CAR

Words and Music by
JONATHAN FOREMAN

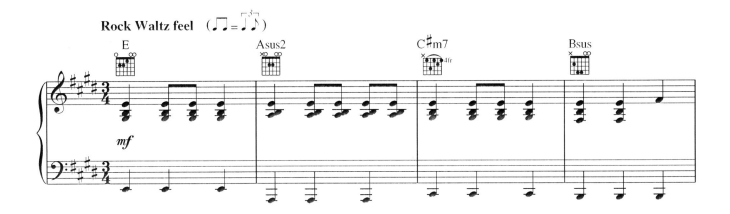

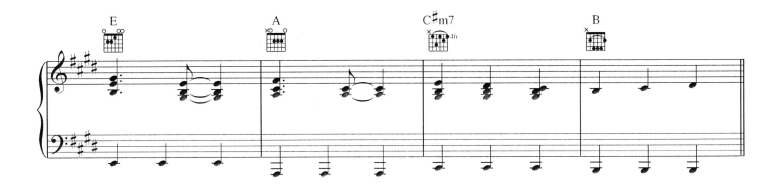

Mike _____ was right _____ when he said I'd put up a fight _____
king _____ of things _____ I've al - ways de - spised. I'm the gin -

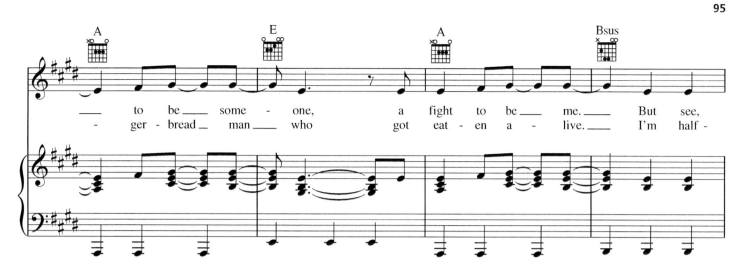

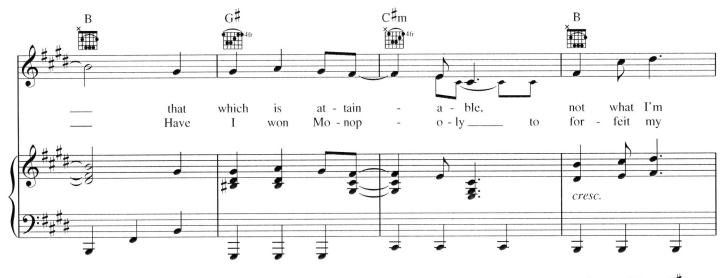

that which is at- tain - a -ble, not what I'm
Have I won Mo - nop - o -ly ____ to for - feit my

cresc.

look - ing for! ___ I've got the com - pa - ny ___ car. ___
soul? But see, ___

f

I'm the one swing - ing at two be - low ___ par. ___ Yeah,

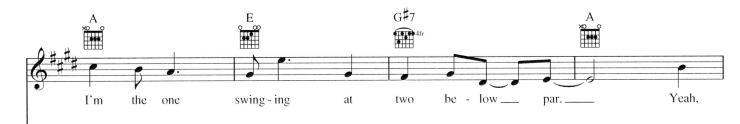

I've be - come one with the ones ___ that I've nev - er be - lieved ___

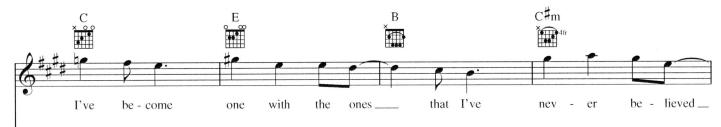

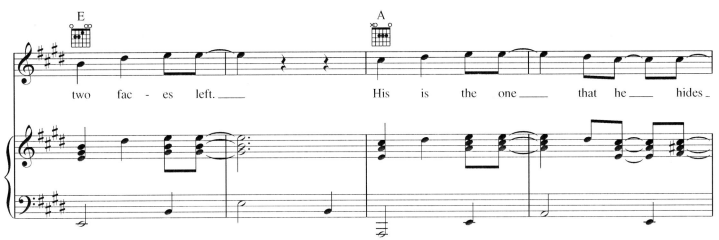

two fac - es left.___ His is the one ___ that he ___ hides __

_____ on the left,___ be - hind that ___

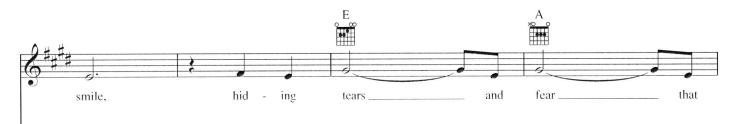

dim. poco a poco

smile, hid - ing tears _____ and fear _____ that

mp

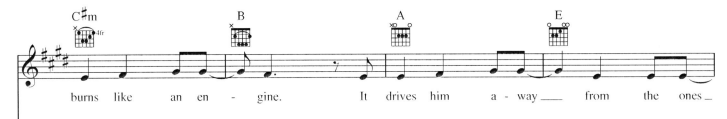

burns like an en - gine. It drives him a - way __ from the ones _

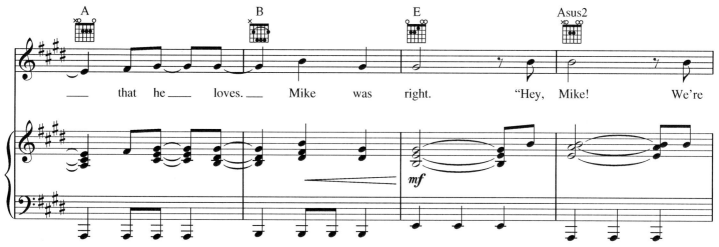

that he ___ loves. ___ Mike was right. "Hey, Mike! We're

one and the same. ___ We're the face - less com - bat - ants in the

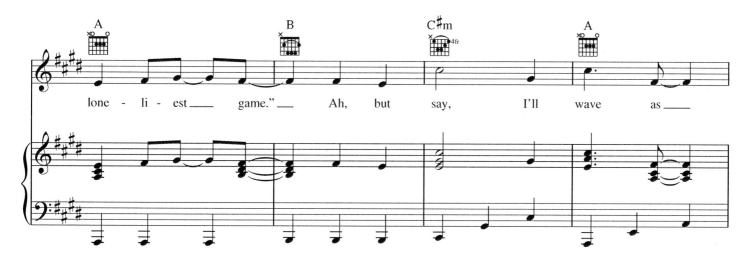

lone - li - est ___ game." ___ Ah, but say, I'll wave as ___

I'm driv - ing by, ___ with that smirk in my ___ eye, ___ yell - ing, "Hey! ___

I'm some - thing, man. Check me out!" I've got the com -

cresc.

f

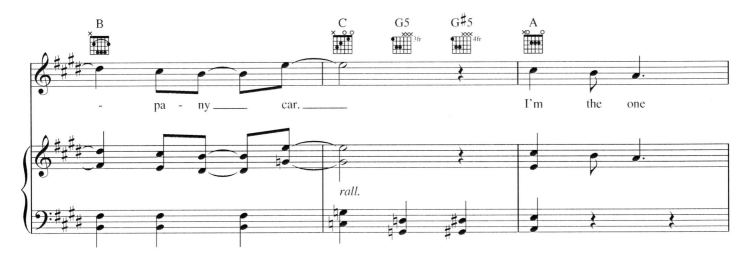

- pa - ny ____ car. ____ I'm the one

rall.

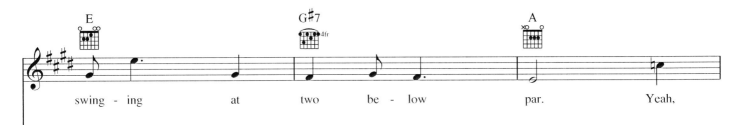

swing - ing at two be - low par. Yeah,

a tempo

I've be - come one with the ones ____ that I've

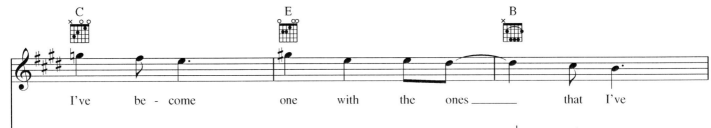

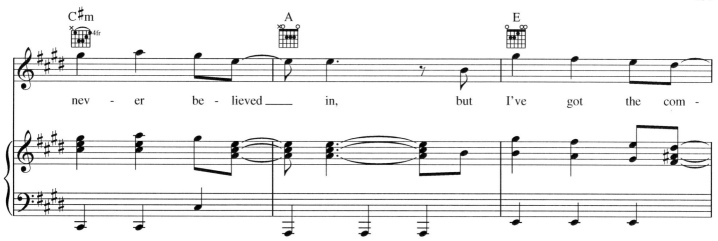

never be-lieved ____ in, but I've got the com -

-pa - ny ____ car. ____ Yeah, check me out! I've got the com -

-pa - ny ____ car. ____ Yeah, check me out! I've got the com -

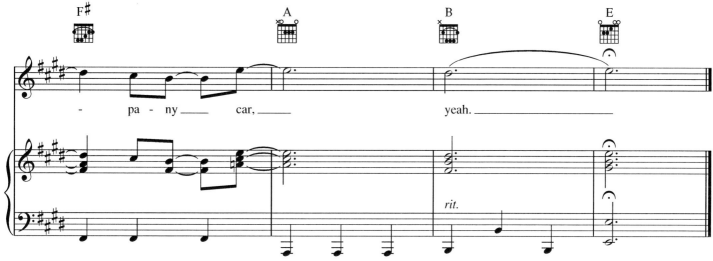

-pa - ny ____ car, ____ yeah. _____

rit.

LONELY NATION

Words and Music by JONATHAN FOREMAN
and TIM FOREMAN

Driving Rock

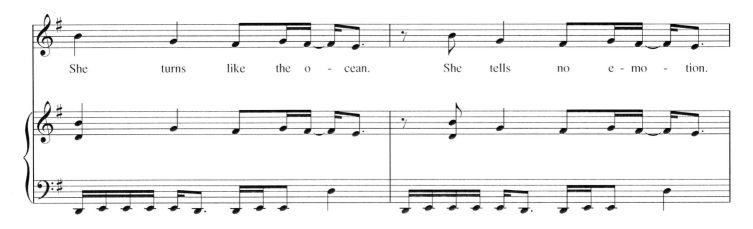

She turns like the o - cean. She tells no e - mo - tion.

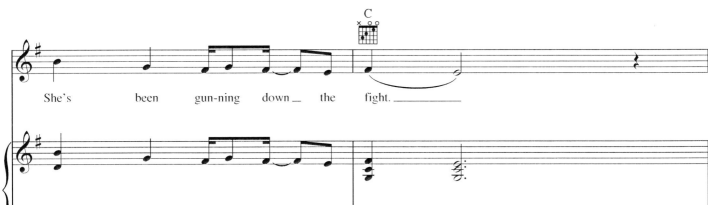

She's been gun-ning down _ the fight. _____

She's just rem - i - nisc - ing; blood, sweat, and one ___ thing's miss - ing.

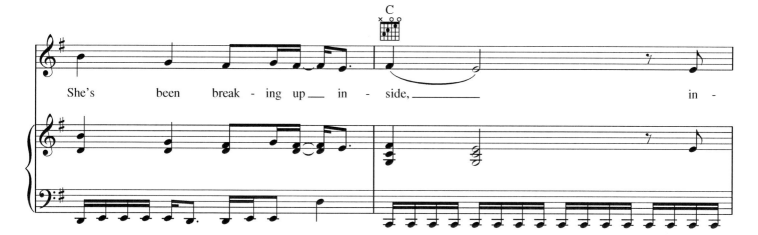

She's been break - ing up ___ in - side, _____ in -

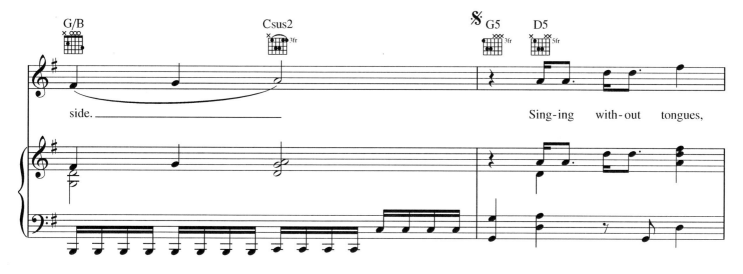

side. _____ Sing-ing with - out tongues,

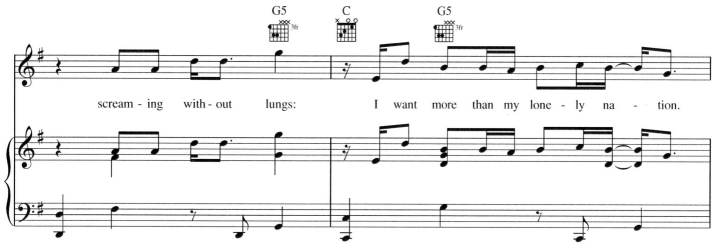

scream - ing with - out lungs: I want more than my lone - ly na - tion.

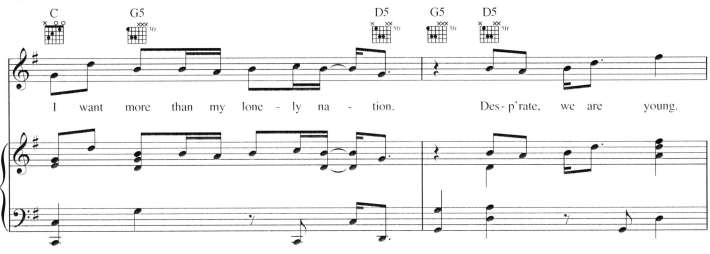

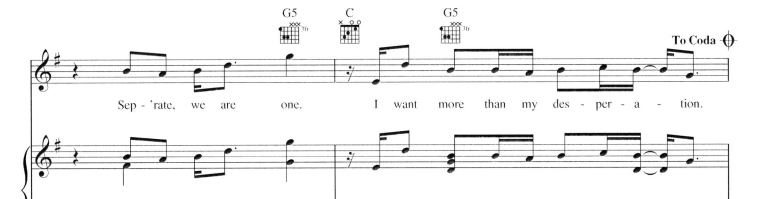

We are the tar - get mar - ket. We set the cor - p'rate tar - get.

We are slaves of what __ we want. _____

We're just numb and a - mused __ and _____ we're just used to bad news __ and

D.S. al Coda

we are slaves of what __ we want. _____

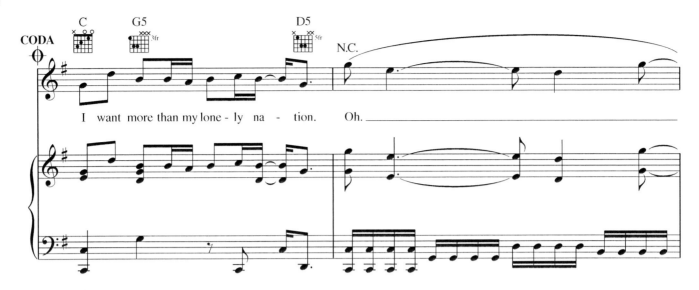

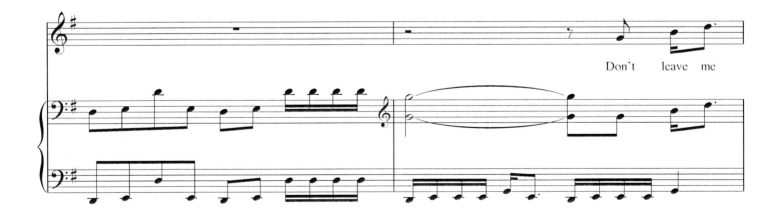

hol - low. I'm tired. Don't leave me

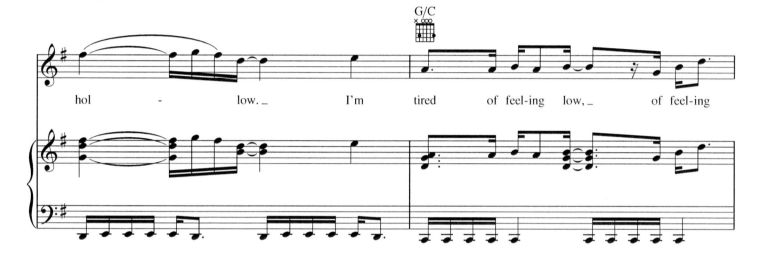

G/C

hol - low.__ I'm tired of feel-ing low,__ of feel-ing

Em7

hol - low. I'm tired of feel-ing low,__ of feel-ing

hol - low.__ I'm tired of feel-ing low,__ of feel-ing

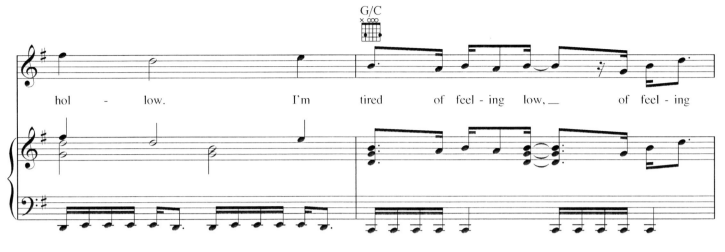

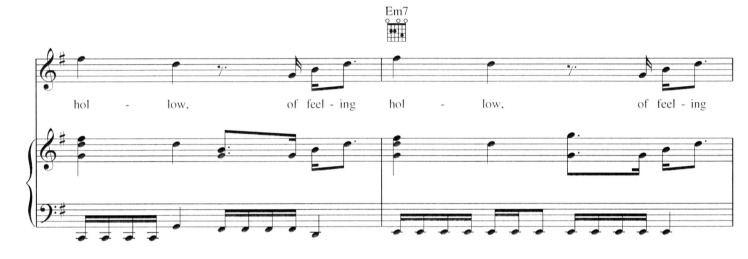

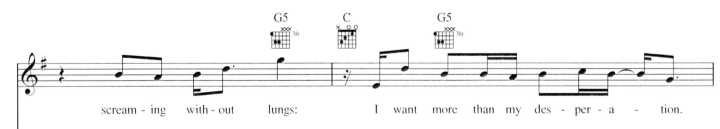

THE SHADOW PROVES THE SUNSHINE

Words and Music by
JONATHAN FOREMAN

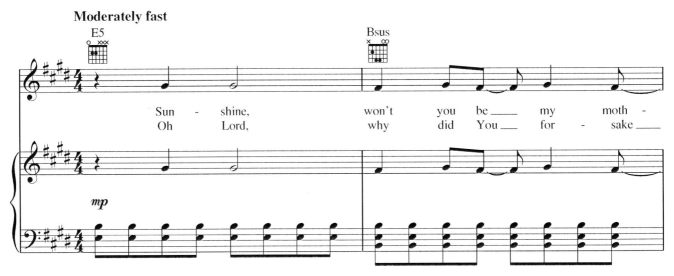

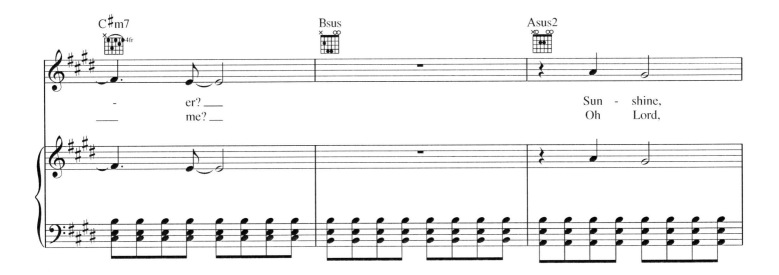

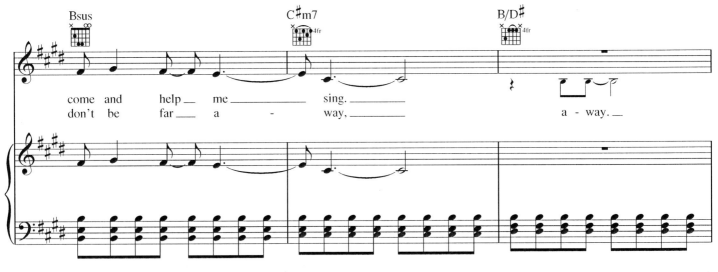

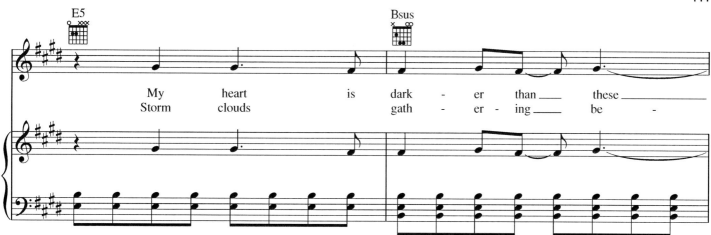

My   heart   is   dark - er   than ___   these _____
Storm   clouds   gath - er - ing ___   be -

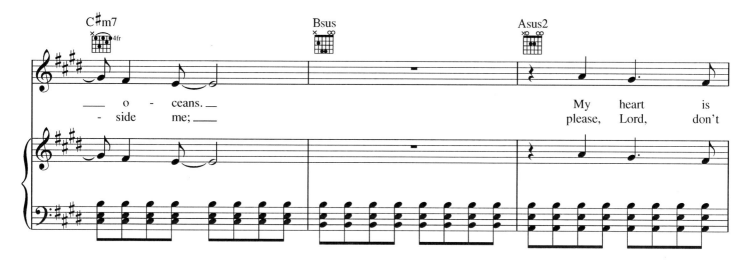

___ o - ceans. ___   My   heart   is
- side   me; ___   please,   Lord,   is   don't

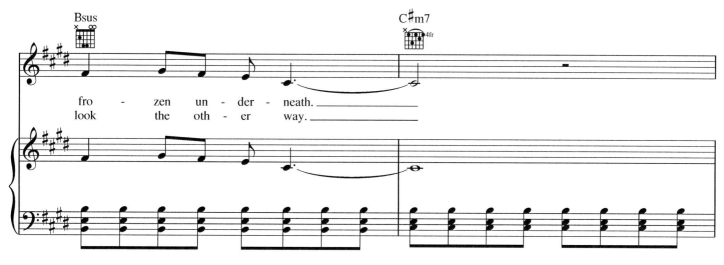

fro - zen   un - der - neath. _____
look   the   oth - er   way. _____

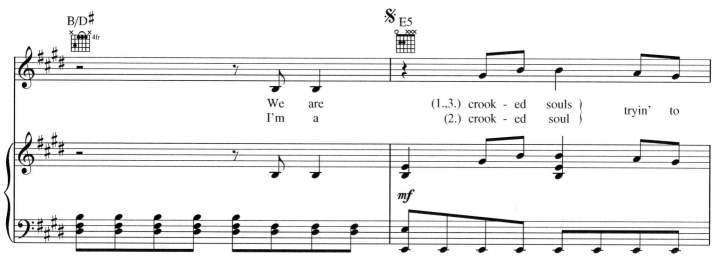

We   are   (1.,3.) crook - ed   souls)   tryin' to
I'm   a   (2.) crook - ed   soul)

mf

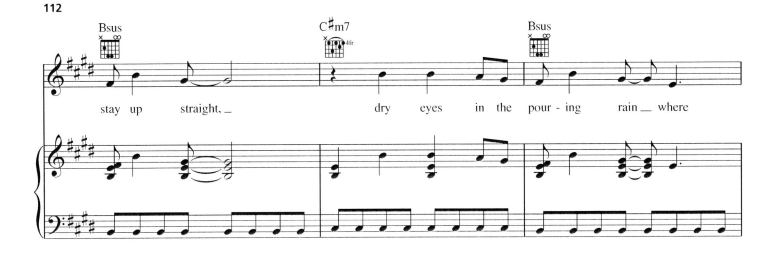

stay up straight, _____ dry eyes in the pour - ing rain ___ where

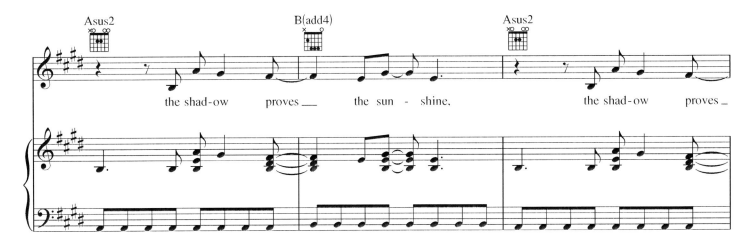

the shad-ow proves ___ the sun - shine, the shad-ow proves _____

_____ the sun - shine. Two scared lit - tle run - a - ways ___

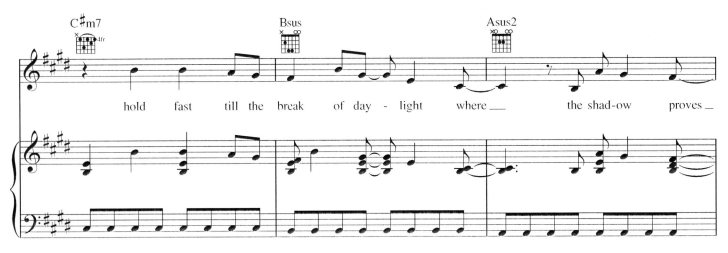

hold fast till the break of day - light where ___ the shad-ow proves ___

the sun - shine, the shad - ow proves ___ the sun - shine.

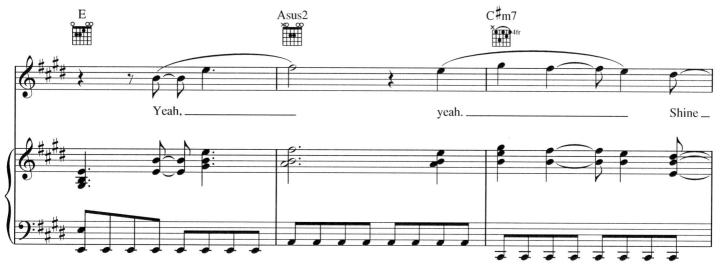

the shad - ow proves ___ the sun - shine.

(sing cue notes 3rd time)

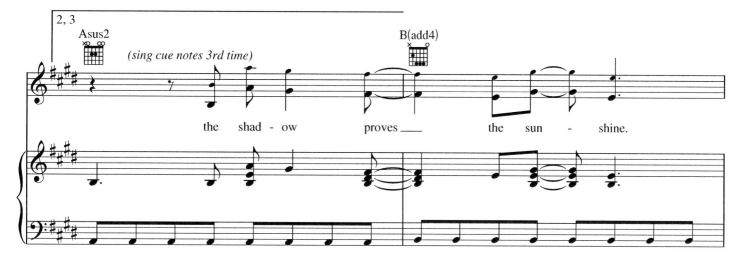

Yeah, ___ yeah. ___ Shine ___

___ on ___ me. ___ Yeah, ___ yeah. ___

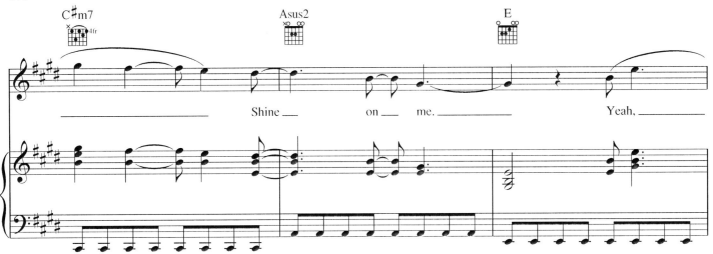

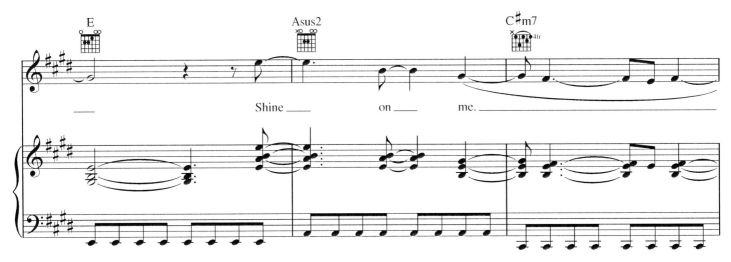

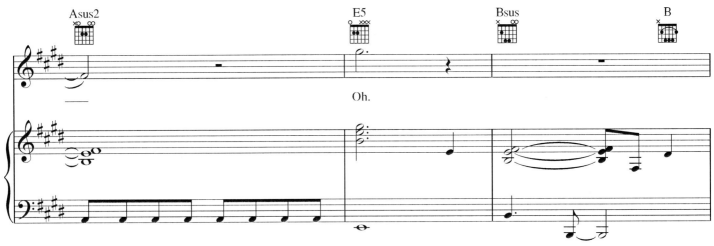

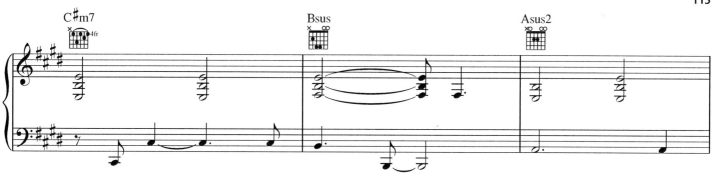

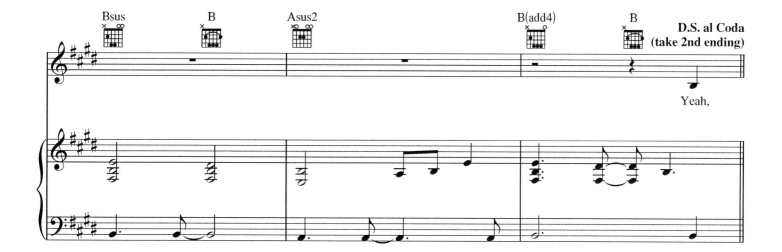

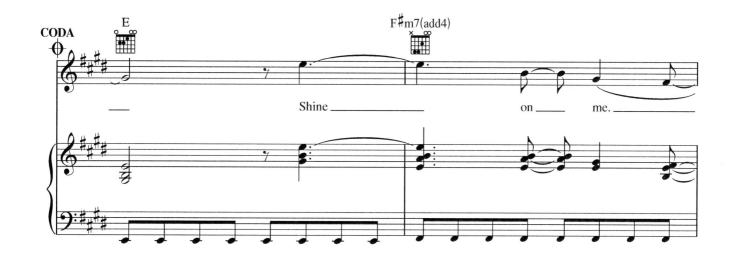

CONCRETE GIRL

Words and Music by
JONATHAN FOREMAN

Moderately slow

Bleed - ing thoughts, __ crack - ing boul -

- der, don't fall o - ver. Fake your laugh -

- ter, burn the tear. __ Sing it loud - er, twist and __

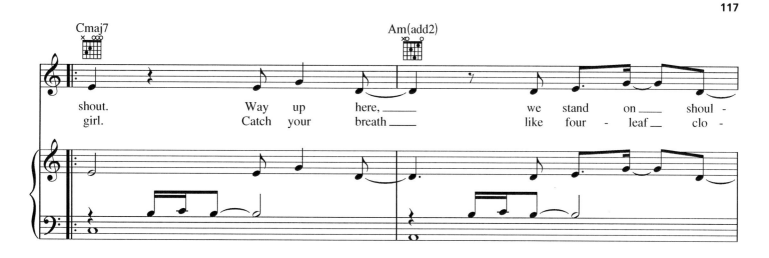

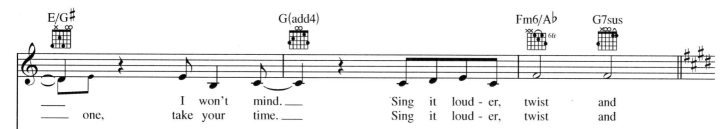

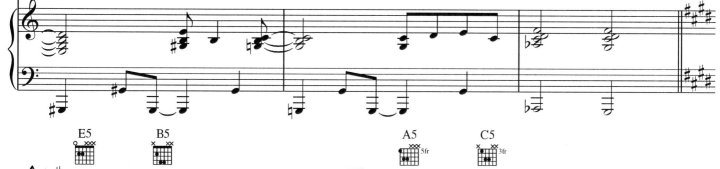

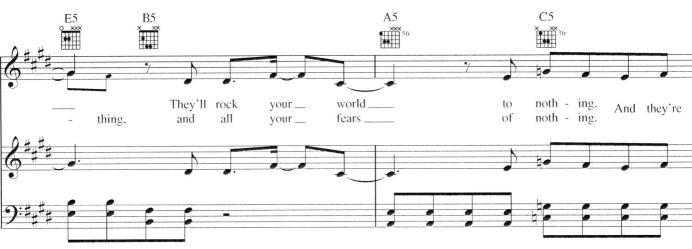

They'll rock your __ world __ to noth - ing. And they're
- thing, and all your __ fears __ of noth - ing.

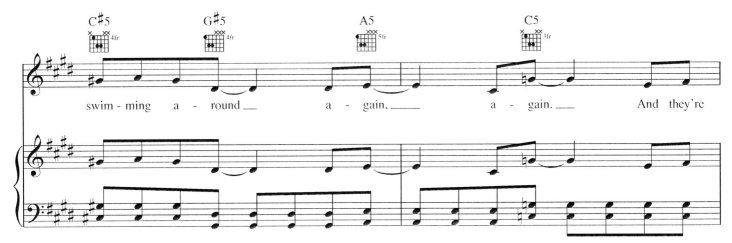

swim - ming a - round __ a - gain, __ a - gain. __ And they're

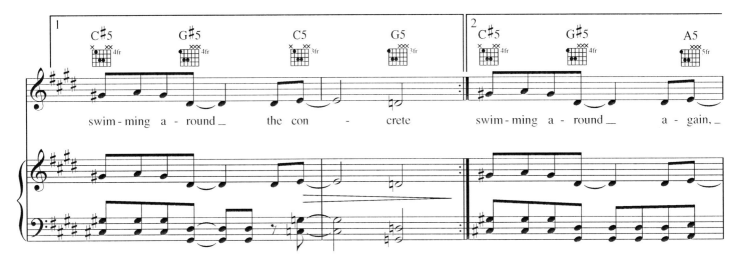

swim - ming a - round __ the con - crete | swim - ming a - round __ a - gain,

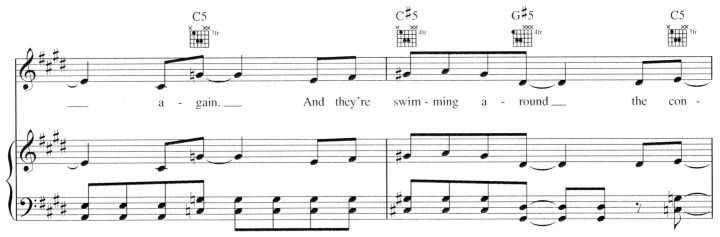

__ a - gain. __ And they're swim - ming a - round __ the con -

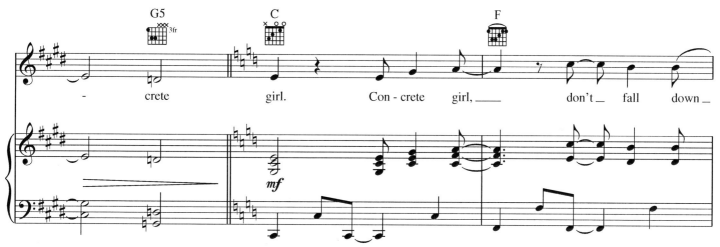

-crete girl. Con - crete girl, ___ don't ___ fall down ___

___ in this bro - ken world ___ a - round ___ you. Con - crete girl, ___

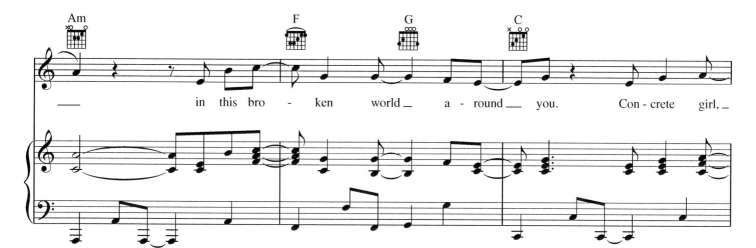

___ don't ___ fall down, ___ don't fall down, ___ my con - crete ___ girl. ___

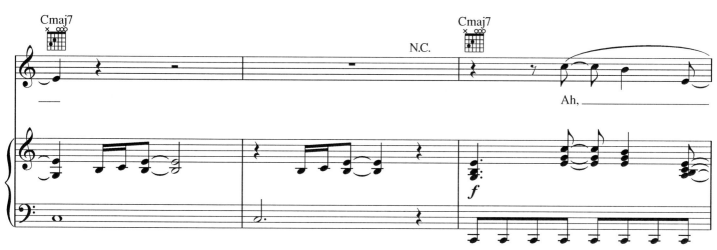

Ah, ___

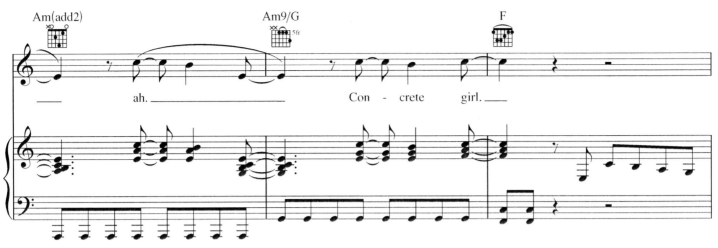

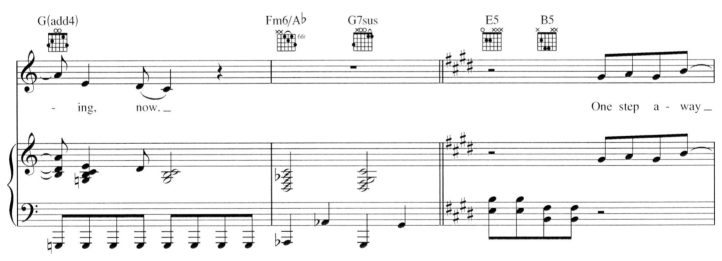

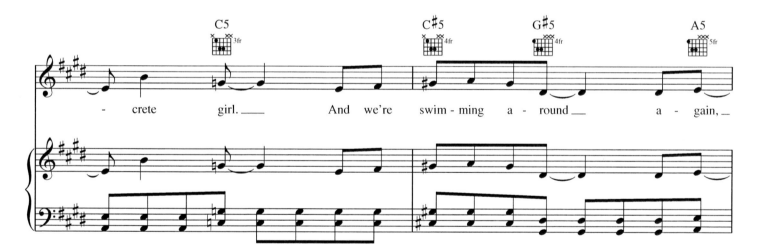

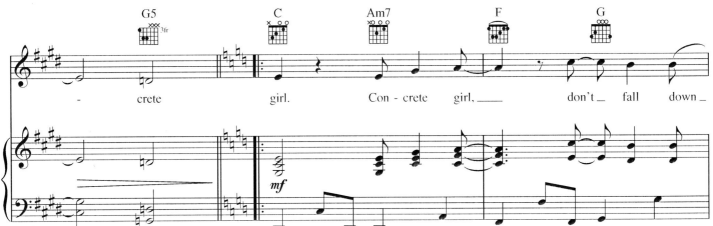

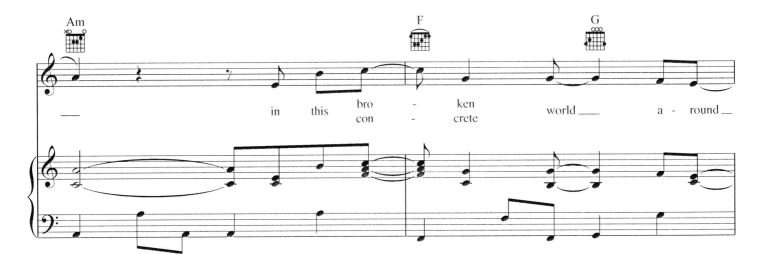

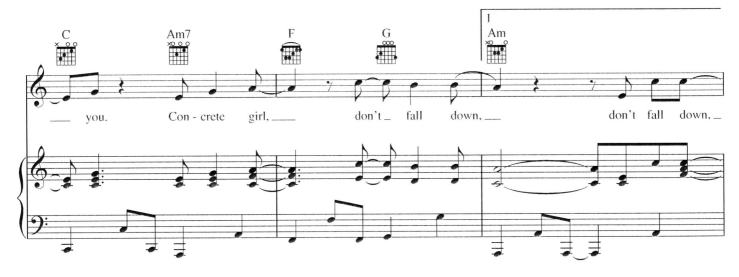

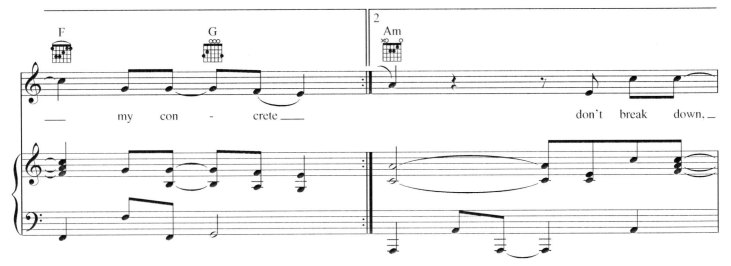

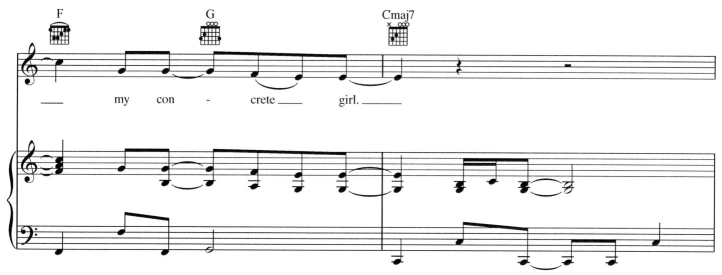

my con - crete girl.

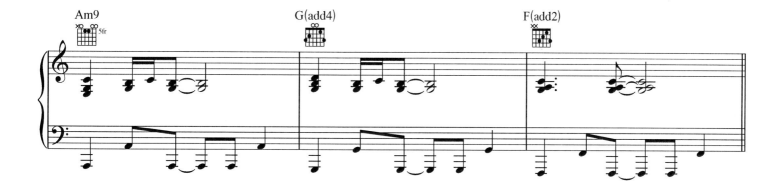

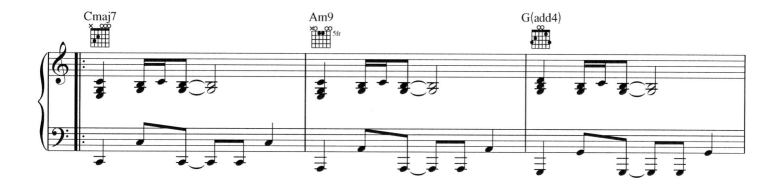

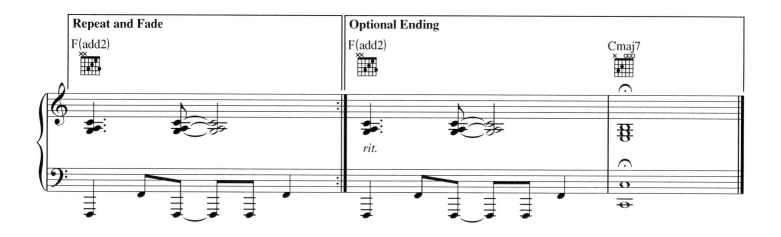

TWENTY-FOUR

Words and Music by
JONATHAN FOREMAN

in twen-ty-fourth place with twen-ty-four

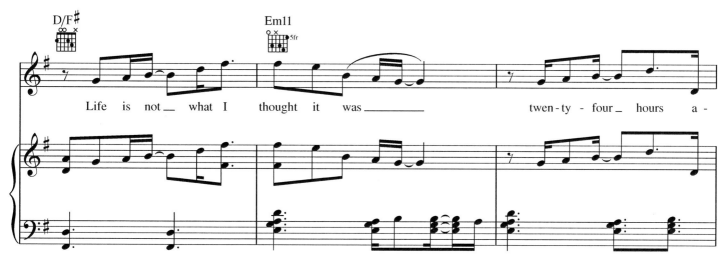

drop - outs _____ at the end of the day. _____

Life is not_ what I thought it was _____ twen-ty-four_ hours a -

go; still I'm sing-ing,_ "Spir - it, take me

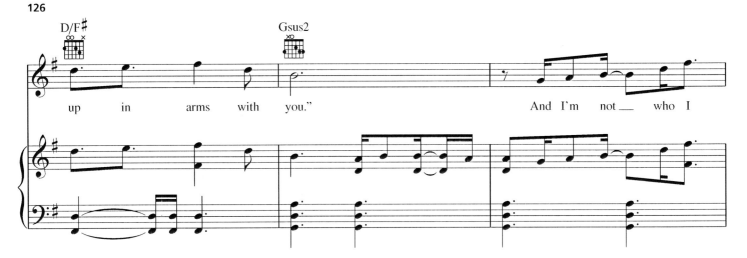

up in arms with you." And I'm not ___ who I

thought I was ___ twen-ty - four ___ hours a - go;

still I'm sing - ing, ___ "Spir - it, take me up in arms with

you." It's twen-ty - four rea - sons ___

to ad - mit that I'm wrong, with all my ex -

cus - es _____ still twen - ty - four strong.

But see, I'm not cop - ping

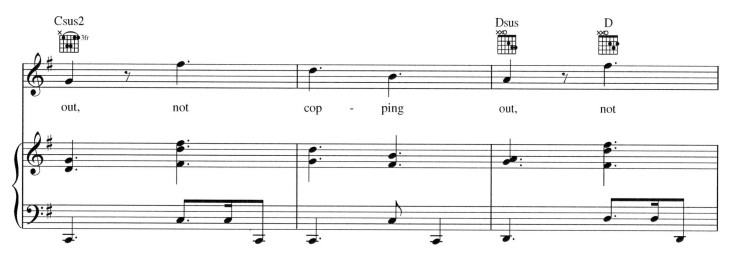

out, not cop - ping out, not

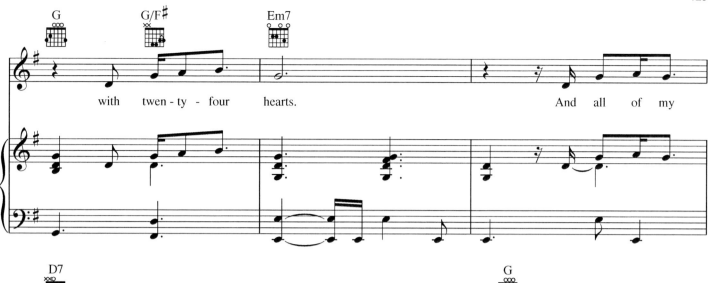

with twen - ty - four hearts. And all of my

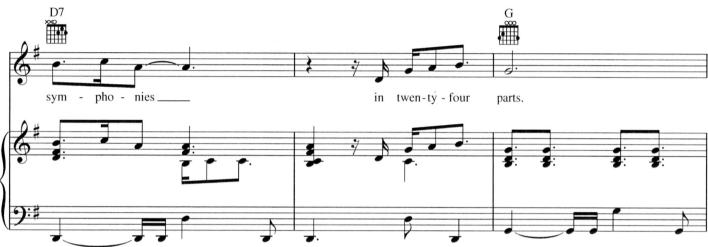

sym - pho - nies ____ in twen - ty - four parts.

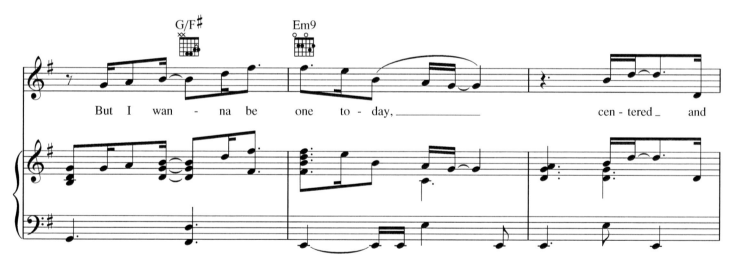

But I wan - na be one to - day, ____ cen - tered _ and

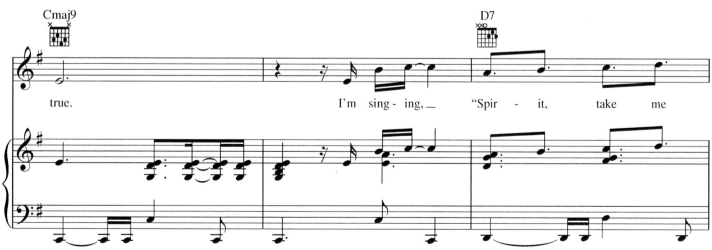

true. I'm sing - ing, _ "Spir - it, take me

up in arms with you." You're rais-ing the dead__ in me.

Oh,_____ oh,_____ I am the sec-ond man. Oh,_____ oh,_____

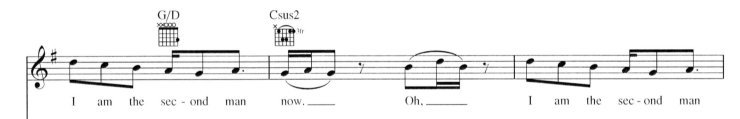

I am the sec-ond man now._____ Oh,_____ I am the sec-ond man

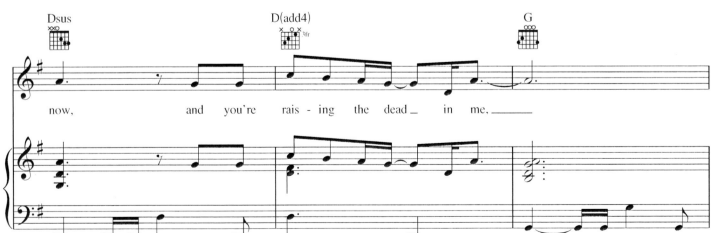

now,_____ and you're rais-ing the dead__ in me,_____

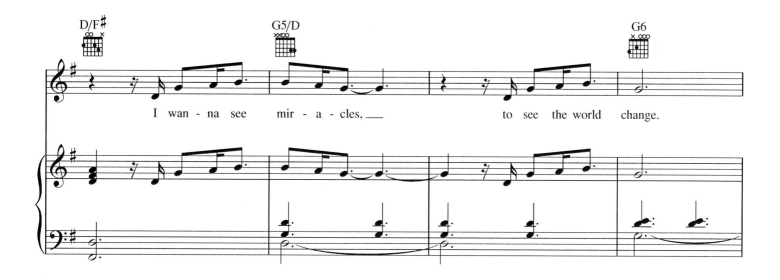

I wan-na see mir-a-cles, ___ to see the world change.

Wres-tled _ the an - gel ___ for more than a name, _

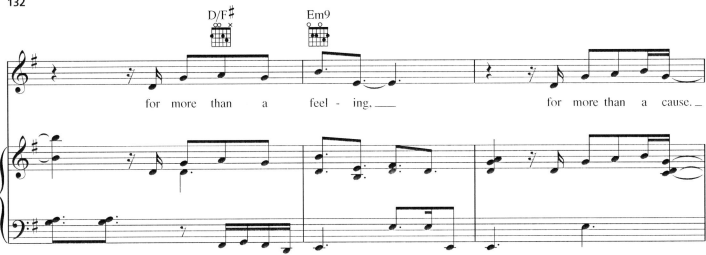

for more than a feel-ing, ___ for more than a cause. __

___ I'm sing-ing, ___ "Spir - it, take me up in arms __ with

you." (And you're rais-ing the dead __ in me.) (Oh, _____ oh, _____

Twen-ty - four o - ceans _____

cop - ping out, not, I'm not _____ cop - ping

I am the sec - ond man now. ____ Oh, _____ I am the sec - ond man

out. _____

now, and you're rais - ing the dead ___ in me.)

Optional Ending

THE BEAUTIFUL LETDOWN

Words and Music by
JONATHAN FOREMAN

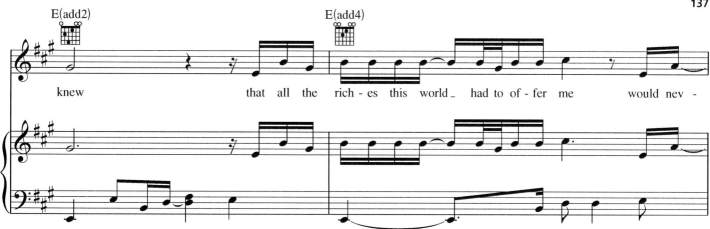

knew _ that all the rich-es this world_ had to of-fer me _ would nev -

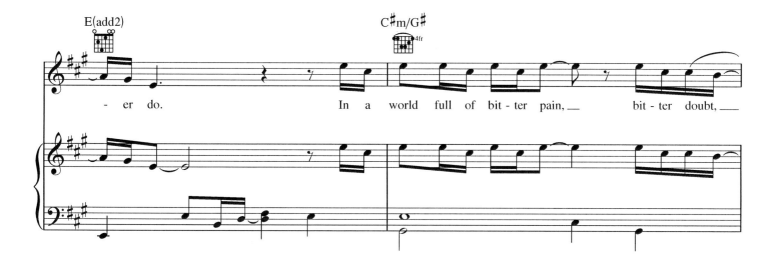

- er do. _ In a world full of bit-ter pain, __ bit-ter doubt, __

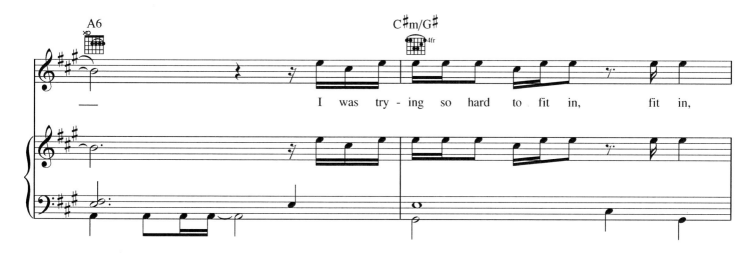

I was try-ing so hard to fit in, _ fit in,

un-til I found out _ that I don't be-long ___ here. _ I don't be-long

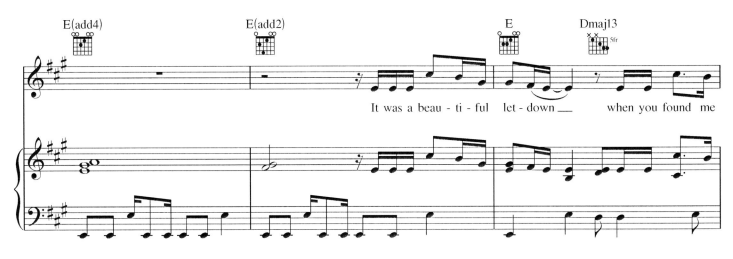

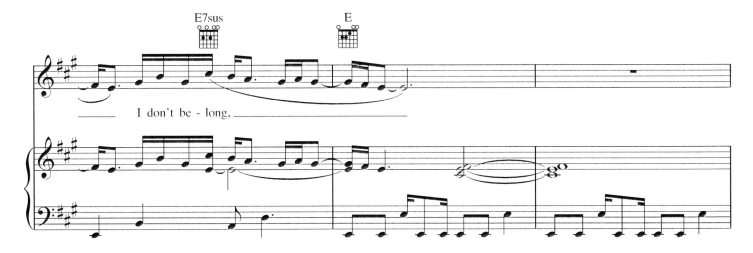

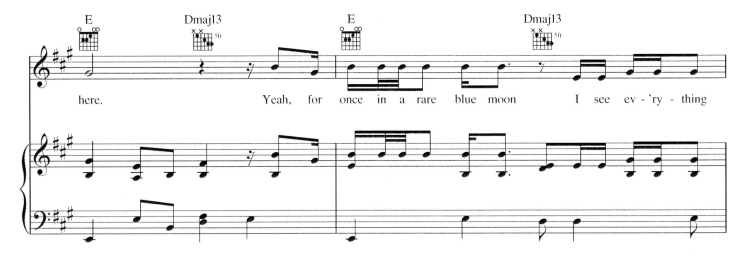

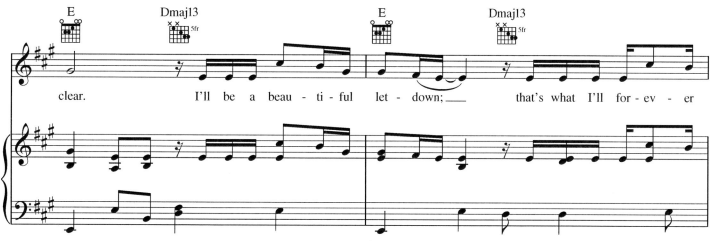

clear.　I'll be a beau - ti - ful let - down;___ that's what I'll for - ev - er

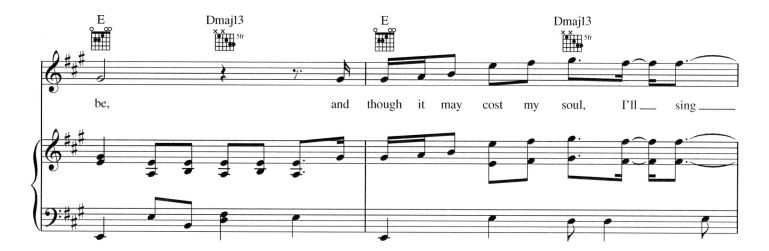

be,　　and though it may cost my soul, I'll___ sing_____

___ for free. ___　We're still chas - ing our tails in the ris - ing

sun, _____　and our dark wa - ter plan - et's still spin - ning in a race where no one

wins and no _ one's won. _ See, I don't be - long _ here. I don't be - long _

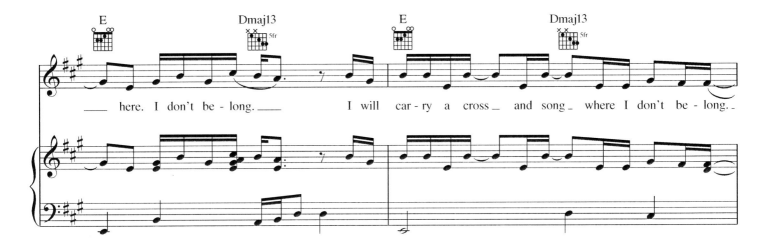

_ here. I don't be - long. _ I will car - ry a cross _ and song _ where I don't be - long. _

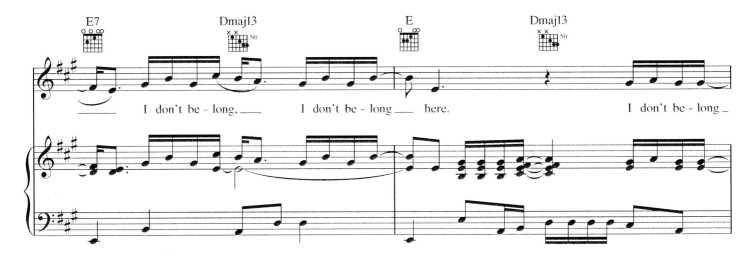

_ I don't be - long, _ I don't be - long _ here. I don't be - long _

_ here. I don't be - long. _ I'm gon - na set sight and set sail _ for the king - dom

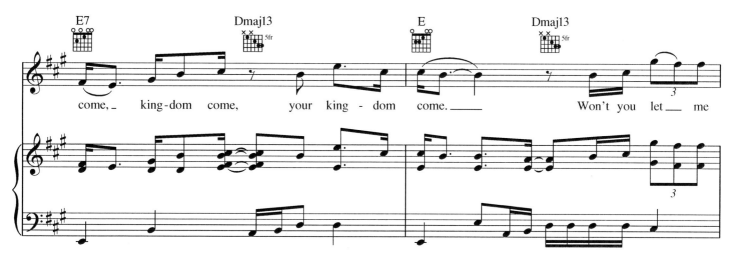

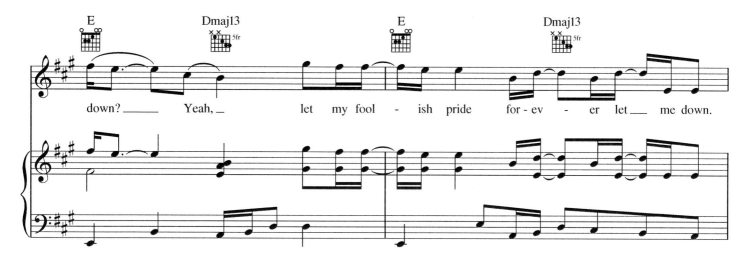

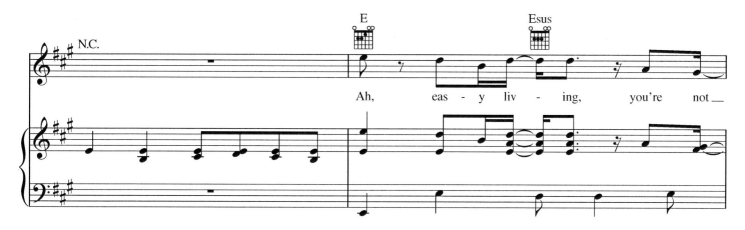

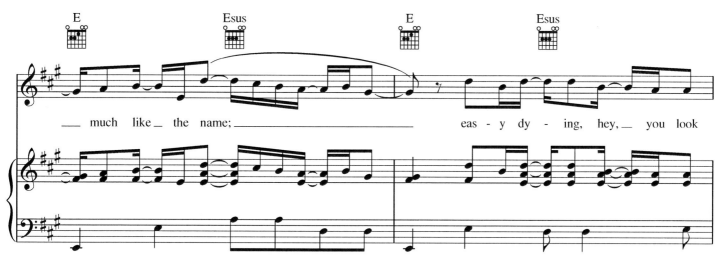

just a - bout_ the same.____ Will you please __ take __ me off __ your list?__

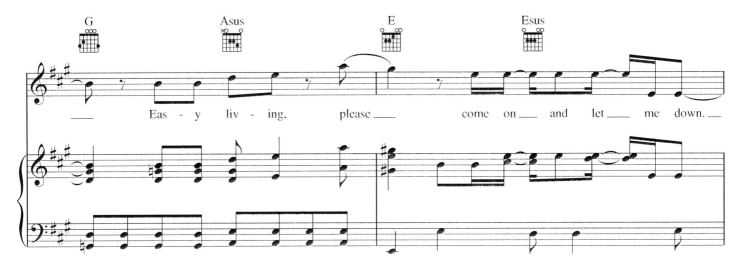

__ Eas - y liv - ing, please ___ come on __ and let __ me down. __

We are a beau - ti - ful let - down, __ pain - ful - ly un -

cool, the church of the drop - outs, the los - ers, the sin - ners, the fail - ures

and the fools. _ Oh, what a beau - ti - ful let - down. _ Are we salt in the

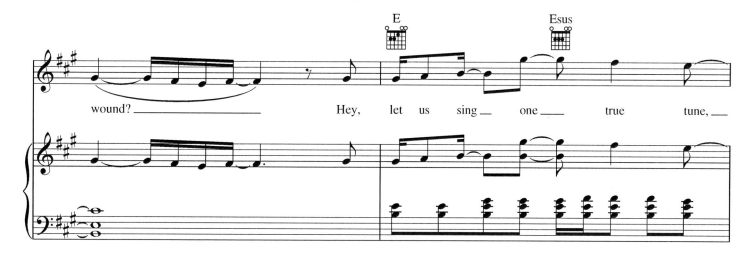

wound? _ Hey, let us sing _ one _ true tune, _

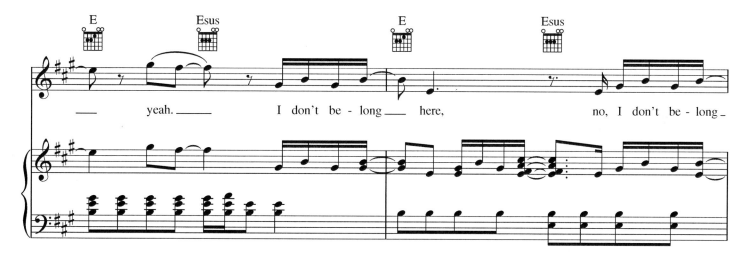

_ yeah. _ I don't be - long _ here, no, I don't be - long _

_ here. Now I don't be - long _ here. Feels like I don't be - long _

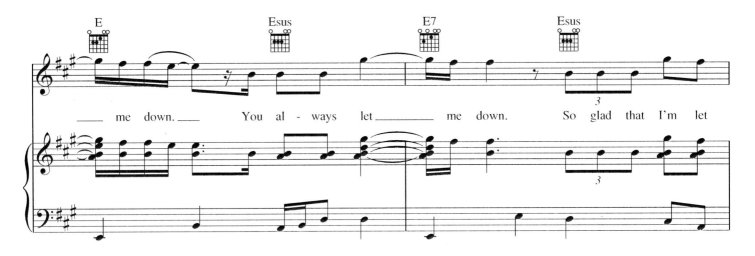

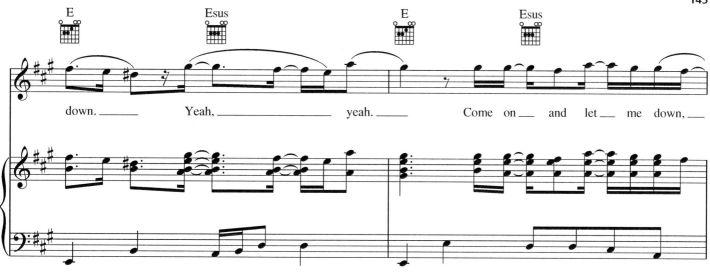

down. _____ Yeah, _____ yeah. _____ Come on __ and let __ me down, __

___ 'cause I don't __ be - long _____ here. Please, __ won't you let __ me down?

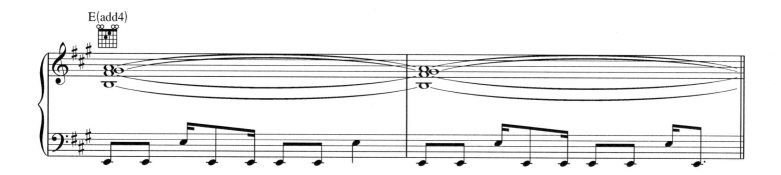

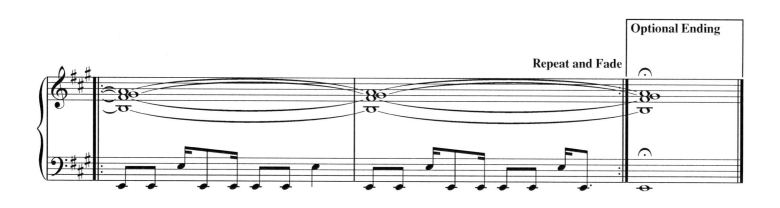

Repeat and Fade   **Optional Ending**

LOVE IS THE MOVEMENT

Words and Music by
JONATHAN FOREMAN

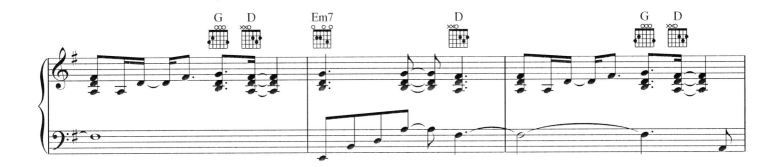

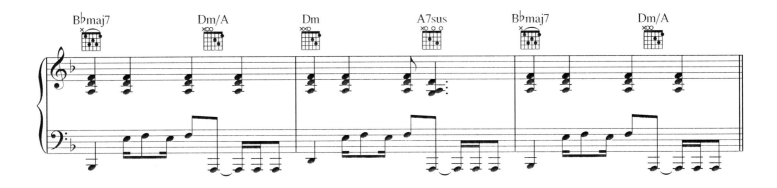

A day in L. A., _____ and mil - lions of
The stars are a - live; _____ they dance to the

fac - es are look - ing for move - ment,
mu - sic of the deep - est e - mo - tion.

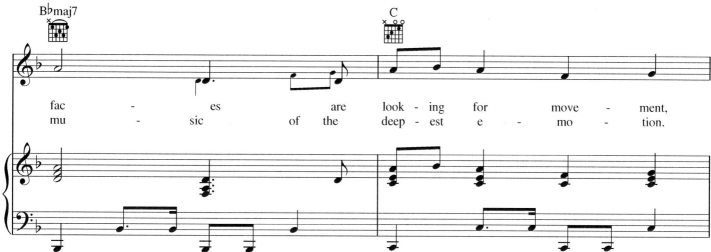

'cause ev - 'ry - thing's stuck and ev - 'ry - thing's __
And all of the world is sing - ing in _____

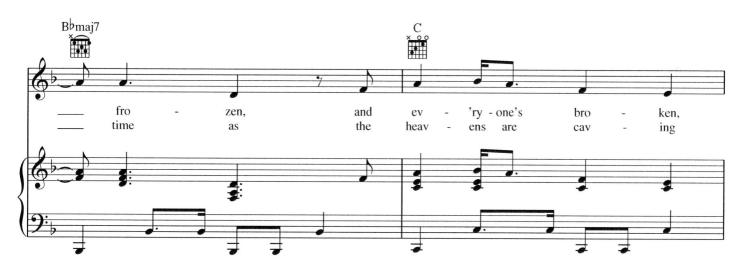

_____ fro - zen, and ev - 'ry - one's bro - ken,
_____ time as the heav - ens are cav - ing

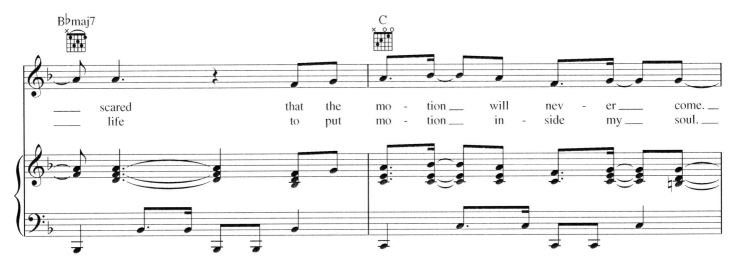

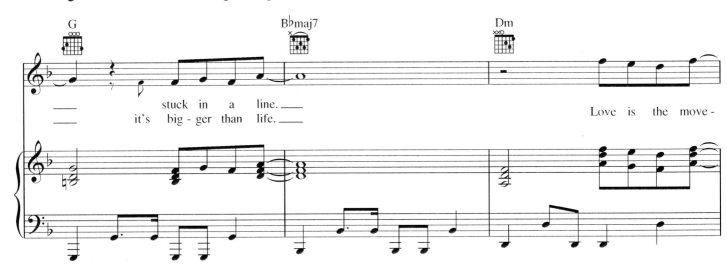

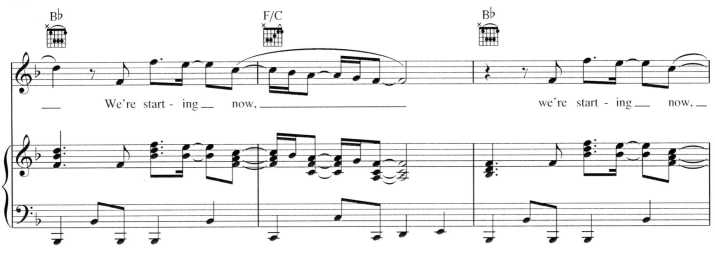

We're start - ing ___ now, _____ we're start - ing ___ now, __

_____ yeah. ___ We're start - ing ___ now. _____

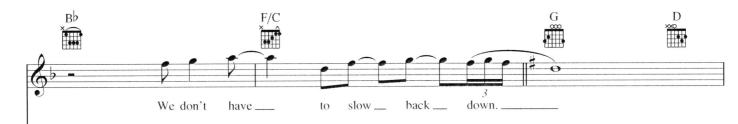

We don't have ___ to slow ___ back ___ down. ___

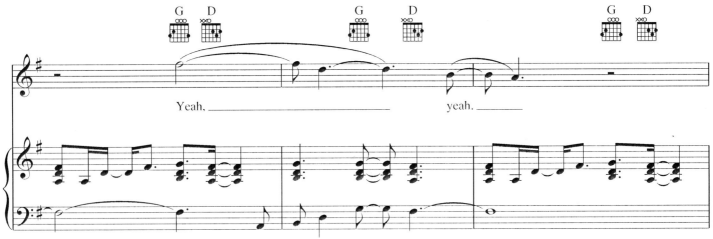

Yeah, _____ yeah. ___

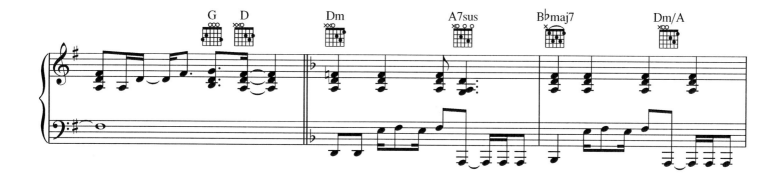

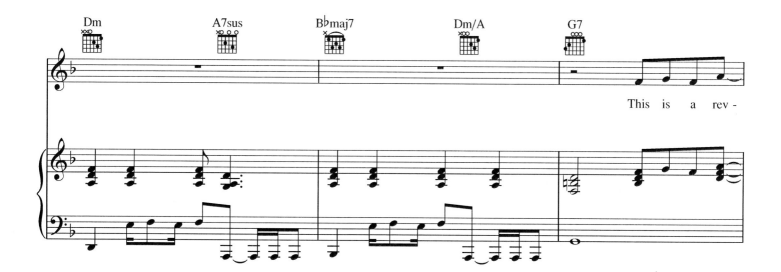

This is a rev -

-o - lu - tion,   this is a rev - o - lu - tion.____

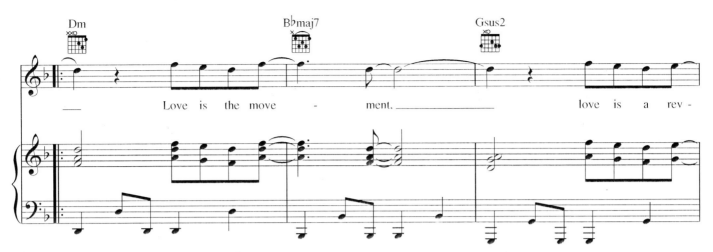